BY AUTHORITY.

NATIONAL,

PATRIOTIC AND TYPICAL AIRS

OF ALL LANDS.

WITH COPIOUS NOTES.

 BY

JOHN PHILIP SOUSA,

BAND MASTER, U. S. M. C.

PHILADELPHIA:

Published by H. COLEMAN, 228 North Ninth St.

ii

To

The Honorable Benjamin F. Tracy

Secretary of the Navy,

THIS WORK

Is Respectfully Inscribed

BY

John Philip Sousa.

NOV 28 1890

Summer Fund

PREFACE.

————>*—*<————

In presenting this volume to the public, the compiler desires to state that he has divided the airs into three classes:—NATIONAL, PATRIOTIC, and TYPICAL. The first embraces those airs, which, either by official decree or by the voice of the people, are known as the principal patriotic airs of their respective countries; the second comprises those which embody words of a patriotic character, or are used at times for patriotic purposes. Under Typical, he has placed those airs which are indigenous to the soil, or the people, and which have come to him as specimens of national music in the broad sense of the term.

It was the compiler's intention to give a few examples of the best modern patriotic songs of our land, but he was compelled to abandon his project. It is popularly supposed that this country is poor in patriotic songs, but instead of finding this to be the fact he discovered such a great number that no volume of ordinary size could contain them. Many of them are excellent compositions and well fitted to serve the purpose of their creation.

Quite a number of the airs came to the compiler without harmonic treatment of any description; he has endeavored to supply that deficiency, but in no instance has he altered the melodic design of any of the airs.

In a few instances the notation does not correspond with that in vogue in America; it has been deemed best not to change it.

The compiler desires to express his sincere thanks to the Honorable James G. Blaine, Secretary, the Honorable Wm. F. Wharton, Assistant Secretary, Dr. F. O. St. Clair, Chief of Consular Bureau, Messrs. H. L. Thomas, J. T. Coughlin and M. M. Shand, all of the Department of State; to Rear-Admiral J. G. Walker and Lieutenant T. B. M. Mason of the Navy; to Mr. A. R. Spofford, Librarian of Congress, Mr. David Hutchinson, the Assistant Librarian, and to all others who have contributed to this work.

JOHN PHILIP SOUSA.

Washington, October 1890.

CONTENTS.

vi

Contents.

Contents.

Contents.

Contents.

x

NAVY DEPARTMENT,

Washington, October 18, 1889.

SPECIAL ORDER:

John Philip Sousa, Bandmaster of the Band of the United States Marine Corps, is hereby directed to compile for the use of the Department the National and Patriotic airs of all Nations.

B. F. TRACY,
Secretary of the Navy.

NAVY DEPARTMENT.

GENERAL ORDER,
No. 374.   *Washington, July 26, 1889.*

In order to insure uniformity, the following routine will be observed at morning and evening colors on board of all men-of-war in commission, and at all Naval Stations:

When a band is present it will play—

At morning colors: "The Star-Spangled Banner."

At evening colors: "Hail Columbia."

All persons present, belonging to the Navy, not so employed as to render it impracticable, will face toward the colors and salute as the ensign reaches the peak or truck in hoisting, or the taffrail or ground in hauling down.

B. F. TRACY,
Secretary of the Navy.

UNITED STATES OF AMERICA.

Hail Columbia!

PATRIOTIC SONG.

Words by Judge Joseph Hopkinson, (1770-1842).   (Evening Colors.)   Music by Fyles.

1. Hail Co-lum-bia, hap-py land! Hail, ye he-roes! heaven-born band! Who fought and bled in
2. Im-mortal pa-triots! rise once more, De-fend your rights; de-fend your shore: Let no rude foe, with

Free-dom's cause, Who fought and bled in Free-dom's cause, And when the storm of war was gone, En-
im-pious hand, Let no rude foe, with im-pious hand, In-vade the shrine where sa-cred lies, Of

" The field music of the revolution consisted mainly of *Yankee Doodle, On the Road to Boston, Rural Felicity, My Dog and Gun,* and *Washington's March,* (the latter composed by the Hon. Francis Hopkinson.) On the occasion of Gen. Washington's attendance at the John St. Theatre in New York, in 1789, a German named Fyles, who was leader of the orchestra, composed a piece in compliment to him and called it the " The President's March," which soon became a popular favorite. The words of *Hail Columbia,* were written by Joseph Hopkinson, son of Francis and Mary Borden Hopkinson, who was born in Philadelphia, November 12, 1770. He was educated at the University of Pennsylvania; studied law with Judge Wilson and Mr. Rawle, and practiced with brilliant success in his native city; was twice elected to Congress from Philadelphia, (1815 and 1817.) In 1828 he was appointed Judge of the District Court for the Eastern District of Pennsylvania, this being the same office which his father held by Washington's appointment. Judge Joseph Hopkinson remained in office till his decease, which took place June 15, 1842. The following is Judge Hopkinson's own account of the origin of " Hail Columbia," written August 24, 1840, for the Wyoming Band, at Wilkesbarre, at their desire.

This song was written in the summer of 1798, when a war with France was thought to be inevitable, Congress then being in session in Philadelphia, deliberating upon that important subject, an act of hostility having actually occurred. The contest between England and France was raging, and the people of the United States were divided into parties for the one side or the other: some thinking that policy and duty required us to take part with republican France, as she was called; others were for our connecting ourselves with England, under the belief that she was the great preservative power of good principles and safe government. The violation of our rights by both belligerents was forcing us from the just and wise policy of President Washington, which was to do equal justice to both; to take part with neither, but to keep a strict and honest neutrality between them. The prospect of a rupture with France was exceedingly offensive to the portion of the people which espoused her cause, and the violence of the spirit of party has never risen higher, I think not so high, as it did at that time, on that question. The theatre was then open in our City. A young man belonging to it, whose talent was good as a singer, was about to take his benefit, I had known him when he was at school. On this acquaintance, he called on me on Saturday afternoon, his benefit being announced for the following Monday. He said he had no boxes taken, and his prospect was, that he should suffer a loss instead of receiving a benefit from the performance; but that if he could get a patriotic song adapted to the tune of the " President's March," (then the popular air), he did not doubt of a full house; that the poets of the theatrical corps had been trying to accomplish it, but were satisfied that no words could be composed to suit the music of the march. I told him I would try for him. He came the next afternoon, and the song, such as it is, was ready for him. It was announced on Monday morning, and the theatre was crowded to excess, and so continued, night after night, for the rest of the season, the song being encored and repeated many times each night, the audience joining in the chorus. It was also sung at night in the streets by large assemblies of citizens, including members of Congress. The enthusiasm was general, and the song was heard, I may say, in every part of the United States. The object of the author was to get up an American spirit, which should be independent of and above the interests, passions and policy of both belligerents, and look and feel exclusively for our honor and our rights. Not an allusion is made either to France or England, or the quarrel between them, or to which was the most in fault in their treatment of us. Of course the song found favor with both parties, at least neither could disavow the sentiments it inculcated. It was truly American, and nothing else—and the patriotic feelings of every American heart responded to it. Such is the history of this song, which has endured infinitely beyond the expectations of the author, and beyond any merit it can boast of, except that of being truly and exclusively patriotic in its sentiments and spirits." *Moore, Nason, Booth's History, et al.*

joyed the peace your val - or won. Let in - de - pend - ence be our boast,
toil and blood the well - earned prize, While of - f'ring peace, sin - cere and just, In

Ev - er mind - ful what it cost, That Ev - er grate - ful for the prize,
heav'n we place a man - ly trust, That truth and jus - tice will pre - vail, And

Let its al - tar reach the skies. Firm, u - nit - ed, let us be, Rally-ing round our
ev - 'ry scheme of bond - age fail.

lib - er - ty; As a band of broth - ers joined, Peace and safe - ty we shall find.

3. Sound, sound the trump of fame!
Let Washington's great name
‖: Ring through the world with loud applause!:‖
Let every clime to freedom dear
Listen with a joyful ear;
With equal skill, with steady power,
He governs in the fearful hour
Of horrid war, or guides with ease
The happier times of honest peace.
Chorus.—Firm, united, &c.

4. Behold the chief, who now commands,
Once more to serve his country stands,—
‖: The rock on which the storm will beat!:‖
But armed in virtue, firm and true,
His hopes are fixed on Heaven and you.
When hope was sinking in dismay,
When gloom obscured Columbia's day,
His steady mind, from changes free,
Resolved on death, or liberty!
Chorus—Firm, united, &c.

UNITED STATES OF AMERICA.

The Star-Spangled Banner.

PATRIOTIC SONG.

Words by Francis Scott Key. (1779–1843.)   (Morning Colors.)   Music by Dr. Samuel Arnold. (1739–1802.)
With an additional verse (5th), by Dr. O. W. Holmes.

Con Spirito.

1. Oh! say can you see, by the dawn's ear - ly light, What so proud - ly we hail'd at the twi - light's last
2. On the shore, dim - ly seen thro' the mist of the deep, Where the foe's haughty host in dread si - lence re -
3. And where is that band, who so vaunt - ing - ly swore, 'Mid the hav - oc of war and the bat - tle's con -

gleaming. Whose stripes and bright stars, thro' the per - il - ous fight, O'er the ram - parts we watch'd, were so gal - lant - ly
pos - es, What is that which the breeze, o'er the tow - er - ing steep, As it fit - ful - ly blows, half con - ceals, half dis -
fu - sion, A home and a coun - try they'd leave us no more? Their blood has wash'd out their foul footstep's po -

streaming; And the rock - et's red glare, the bombs bursting in air, Gave proof thro' the night that our flag was still there!
clos - es? Now it catch - es the gleam of the morning's first beam, In full glo - ry re - flect - ed, now shines in the stream.
lu - tion; No ref - uge could save the hire - ling and slave From the ter - ror of flight or the gloom of the grave.

CHORUS.

1. Oh! say, does that star - spangled ban - ner yet wave, O'er the land of the free and the home of the brave!
2. 'Tis the star - spangled ban - ner, oh! long may it wave, O'er the land of the free and the home of the brave!

3. And the star - spangled ban - ner in tri - umph shall wave, O'er the land of the free and the home of the brave!
4. And the star - spangled ban - ner in tri - umph shall wave, While the land of the free is the home of the brave!

5. And the star - spangled ban - ner in tri - umph shall wave, While the land of the free is the home of the brave!

4.

Oh! thus be it ever when freemen shall stand.
  Between their loved home and the war's desolation,
Blest with vict'ry and peace, may the heav'n-rescued land,
  Praise the Pow'r that hath made and preserved us a nation.
Then conquer we must, when our cause it is just,
And this be our motto, "In God is our trust."—*Chorus.*

5.

When our land is illum'd with liberty's smile,
  If a foe from within strike a blow at her glory,
Down, down with the traitor, that dares to defile
  The flag of her stars and the page of her story!
By the millions unchain'd who our birth-right have gain'd,
We will keep her bright blazon forever unstain'd.—*Chorus.*

"The music of the Star-Spangled Banner was composed by Dr. Samuel Arnold, for the old drinking song, 'To Anacreon in Heaven.' It was first used as a patriotic song in this country to the ode 'Adams and Liberty,' written by Robert Treat Paine, born in Taunton, Mass., Dec. 9, 1773, died Nov. 13, 1811."—*Horton, et al.*

The compiler has in his possession an old English volume in which "To Anacreon in Heaven" is given as follows:

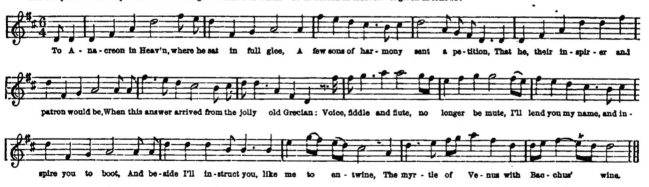

To A - na - creon in Heav'n, where he sat in full glee, A few sons of har - mony sent a pe - tition, That he, their in - spir - er and patron would be, When this answer arrived from the jolly old Grecian: Voice, fiddle and flute, no longer be mute, I'll lend you my name, and in - spire you to boot, And be - side I'll in - struct you, like me to en - twine, The myr - tle of Ve - nus with Bac - chus' wine.

"The words of the *Star Spangled Banner* were written by Francis Scott Key, son of John Ross Key, an officer in the Revolutionary army. He was born Aug. 1, 1779, and died Jan. 11, 1843. The words were written Sep. 14, 1814, under the following circumstances. After burning Washington, the British advanced towards Baltimore, and were met by a smaller number of Americans, most of whom were captured and taken to the large fleet, then preparing to attack Fort McHenry. Among the prisoners taken at Bladensburg, was a Doctor Beanes, an intimate friend of Mr. Key. Hoping to intercede for the Doctor's release, Mr. Key, with a flag of truce, started in a sail-boat for the Admiral's (Cockburn) vessel. Here he was detained in his boat, moored from the stern of the flag-ship, during the terrible bombardment of twenty-five hours, and at last, seeing the "Star-Spangled Banner" still waving, then, as his fashion was, he snatched an old letter from his pocket, and laying it on a barrel-head, gave vent to his delight in the spirited song which he entitled "The Defense of Fort McHenry." "The Star-Spangled Banner" was printed within a week in the Baltimore Patriot, under the title of "The Defense of Fort McHenry," and found its way immediately into the camps of our army. Ferdinand Durang, who belonged to a dramatic company, and had played in a Baltimore theatre with John Howard Payne, read the poem effectively to the soldiers encamped in that city, who were expecting another attack. They begged him to set the words to music, and he hunted up the old air of "Adams and Liberty," set the words to it, and sang it to the soldiers who caught it up amid tremendous applause."—*Johnson, Our Familiar Songs, Anderson's History, Nason's Monogram, et al.*

UNITED STATES OF AMERICA.

Columbia, the Gem of the Ocean.

PATRIOTIC SONG.

Written and Composed by David T. Shaw.

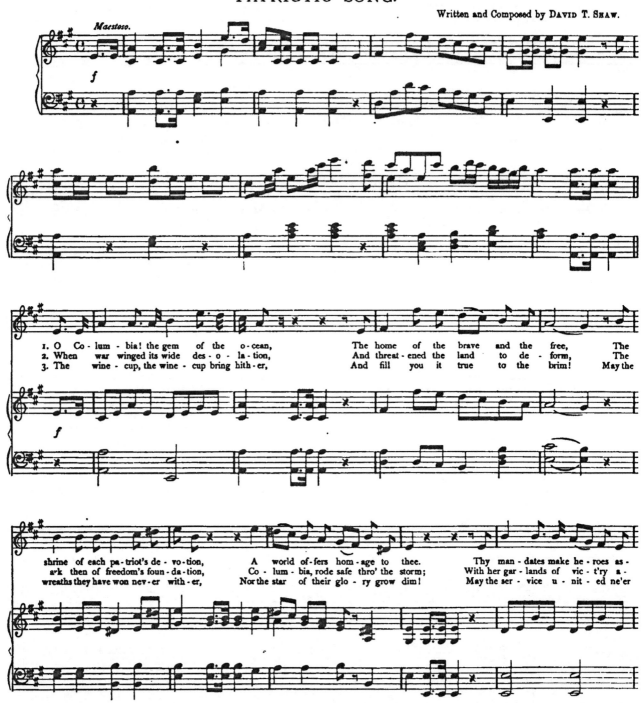

Maestoso.

1. O Co - lum - bia! the gem of the o - cean, The home of the brave and the free, The
2. When war winged its wide des - o - la - tion, And threat - ened the land to de - form, The
3. The wine - cup, the wine - cup bring hith - er, And fill you it true to the brim! May the

shrine of each pa - triot's de - vo - tion, A world of - fers hom - age to thee. Thy man - dates make he - roes as -
ark then of freedom's foun - da - tion, Co - lum - bia, rode safe thro' the storm; With her gar - lands of vic - t'ry a -
wreaths they have won nev - er with - er, Nor the star of their glo - ry grow dim! May the ser - vice u - nit - ed ne'er

"When in America, I made inquiry regarding the author of this song, (The Red, White and Blue). My reason for making these inquiries was that, about twenty or twenty-five years ago, I first heard in 'the old country' this same song sung in our street, but somewhat varied.

The British song sang thus:

'Britannia, the pride of the Ocean,
The home of the brave and the free,
The shrine of each sailor's devotion,
What land can compare unto thee.'

It is quite clear one version must be taken from the other, for each is appropriate only to the eastern or western side of the Atlantic."—*Paul Ward, in Notes and Queries, July 1870.*

The title of the song given in an edition published in Baltimore, in 1852, is "Columbia, the Land of the Brave." Nason in his Monagram says, "Columbia the Gem of the Ocean, by David T. Shaw, and set to the English tune of 'The Red, White and Blue.'" * * * *

UNITED STATES OF AMERICA.

Yankee Doodle.

PATRIOTIC AIR.

(THE ORIGINAL WORDS.)

Allegretto.

1. Fa - ther and I went down to camp, A - long with Cap - tain Good - win, And
2. And there was Cap - tain Wash - ing - ton, Up - on a slap - ping stal - lion, And
3. And then the feath - ers on his hat, They looked so 'tar - nal fun - ny I
4. And then they had a swamp - ing gun, As big as a log of ma - ple,

there we saw the men and boys, As thick as has - ty pud - din'. Yan - kee Doo - dle keep it up,
giv - ing or - ders to his men, I guess there was a mil - lion.
want - ed pes - ke - ly to get, To give to my Je - mi - na.
On a deuc - ed lit - tle cart, A load for fa - ther's cat - tle.

Yan - kee Doo - dle dan - dy, Mind the mu - sic and the step, And with the girls be hand - y.

5. And every time they fired it off
   It took a horn of powder;
   It made a noise like father's gun,
   Only a nation louder.

6. I went as near to it myself
   As Jacob's underpinin',
   And father went as near again—
   I thought the deuce was in him.

7. (It scared me so I ran the streets,
   Nor stopped as I remember,
   Till I got home, and safely locked
   In granny's little chamber.)

8. And there I see a little keg,
   Its heads were made of leather,
   They knocked upon 't with little sticks,
   To call the folks together.

9. And there they'd fife away like fun,
   And play on corn stalk fiddles,
   And some had ribbons red as blood,
   All bound around their middles.

10. The troopers too, would gallop up,
    And fire right in our faces;
    It scared me almost half to death
    To see them run such races.

11. Uncle Sam came there to change
    Some pancakes and some onions,
    For 'lasses cakes to carry home
    To give his wife and young ones.

12. But I can't tell you half I see,
    They kept up such a smother;
    So I took my hat off, made a bow,
    And scampered home to mother.

The following version was written by Gen. Geo. P. Morris, of Philadelphia, born 1802, died 1864.

1. Once on a time old Johnny Bull flew in a raging fury,
And swore that Jonathan should have no trials, sir, by jury,—
That no elections should be held across the briny waters;
And now said he, "I'll tax the tea of all his sons and daughters."
Then down he sate in burly state, and blustered like a grandee,
And in derision made a tune called, "Yankee doodle dandy."
"Yankee doodle—these are facts—Yankee doodle dandy:
My son of wax, your tea I'll tax; you—Yankee doodle dandy

2. John sent the tea from o'er the sea, with heavy duties rated,
But whether hyson or bohea I never heard it stated.
Then Jonathan to pout began—he laid a strong embargo—
"I'll drink no tea, by Jove!" so he threw overboard the cargo.
Then Johnny sent a regiment, big words and looks to bandy,
Whose martial band, when near the land, played "Yankee doodle dandy."
Yankee doodle—keep it up—Yankee doodle dandy—
I'll poison with a tax your cup; you—"Yankee doodle dandy."

3. A long war then they had, in which John was at last defeated,
And "Yankee doodle" was the march to which his troops retreated.
'Cute Jonathan, to see them fly, could not restrain his laughter,
"That tune," said he, "suits to a T, I'll sing it ever after."
Old Johnny's face, to his disgrace, was flushed with beer and brandy,
E'en while he swore to sing no more this "Yankee doodle dandy."
Yankee doodle—ho, ha, he—Yankee doodle dandy;
We kept the tune, but not the tea—Yankee doodle dandy.

4. I've told you now the origin of this most lively ditty,
Which Johnny Bull dislikes as "dull and stupid"—what a pity!—
With "Hail Columbia" it is sung, in chorus full and hearty,—
On land and main we breathe the strain, John made for his tea party.
No matter how we rhyme the words, the music speaks them handy,
And where's the fair can't sing the air of "Yankee doodle dandy!"
Yankee doodle, firm and true—Yankee doodle dandy;
Yankee doodle, doodle doo, Yankee doodle dandy.

"In looking over an old file of the Albany Statesman, edited by N. H. Carter, Esq., we meet with the following interesting note, respecting the origin of the tune "Yankee Doodle," the words of which were published in the Collections for May. It is known as a matter of history, that in the early part of 1755, great exertions were made by the British Ministry, at the head of which was the illustrious Earl of Chatham, for the reduction of the French power in the provinces of the Canadas. To carry the object into effect, General Amherst, referred to in the letters of Junius, was appointed to the command of the British army in North Western America; and the British colonies in America were called upon for assistance, and contributed with alacrity their several quotas of men, to effect the grand object of British enterprise. It is a fact still in the recollection of some of our oldest inhabitants, that the British army lay encamped, in the summer of 1755, on the eastern bank of the Hudson, a little south of the city of Albany, on the ground now belonging to John I. Van Rensselar, Esq. To this day vestiges of their encampment remain; and after a lapse of sixty years, when a great proportion of the actors of those days have passed away like shadows from the earth, the inquisitive traveller can observe the remains of the ashes, the places where they boiled their camp kettles. It was this army, that, under the command of Abercrombie, was foiled, with a severe loss, in the attack on Ticonderoga, where the distinguished Howe fell at the head of his troops, in an hour that history has consecrated to his fame. In the early part of June, the eastern troops began to pour in, company after company, and such a motley assemblage of men never before thronged together on such an occasion, unless an example may be found in the ragged regiment of Sir John Falstaff, of right merry and facetious memory. 'It would,' said my worthy ancestor, who relates to me the story, 'have relaxed the gravity of an anchorite, to have seen the descendants of the Puritans, marching through the streets of our ancient city, to take their station on the left of the British army—some with long coats, some with short coats, and others with no coats at all, in colors as varied as the rainbow, some with their hair cropped, like the army of Cromwell, and others with wigs whose curls flowed with grace around their shoulders. Their march, their accoutrements and the whole arrangement of the troops, furnished matter of amusement to the wits of the British army. The music played the airs of two centuries ago, and the tout ensemble, upon the whole, exhibited a sight to the wondering strangers that they had been unaccustomed to in their own land. Among the club of wits that belonged to the British army, there was a physician attached to the staff, by the name of Doctor Schackburg, who combined with the science of the surgeon, the skill and talent of a musician. To please brother Jonathan, he composed a tune, and with much gravity recommended it to the officers, as one of the most celebrated airs of martial music. The joke took, to the no small amusement of the British Corps. Brother Jonathan exclaimed it was 'nation fine, and in a few days nothing was heard in the provincial camp but the air of Yankee Doodle. Little did the author or his co-adjutors then suppose, that an air made for the purpose of levity and ridicule, should ever be marked for such high destinies; in twenty years from that time, our National march, inspired the hearts of the heroes of Bunker Hill, and less than thirty, Lord Cornwallis and his army marched into the American lines to the tune of Yankee Doodle."—Letter in Farmer and Moore's Historical Collection for 1824.

"This tune, however, was not original with Dr. Schackburg. He made it from an old song which can be traced back to the reign of Charles I.; a song which has in its day been used for a great variety of words. One of the songs, written in ridicule of the Protector, began with this line:— 'The Roundheads and the Cavaliers.' Another set of words to the same tune was entitled 'Nankee Doodle.' and ran thus:—

'Nankee Doodle came to town
Upon a little pony,
With a feather in his hat,
Upon a macaroni.'

The first American parody upon the original which we have seen was entitled 'Lydia Fisher.' An aged and respectable lady, born in New England, says she remembers it well, and that it was a common song, long before the Revolution. It was also a favorite New England jig.

Before the war it was customary to sing the tune with various impromptu verses, such as:—

'Lydia Locket lost her pocket,
Lydia Fisher found it;
Not a bit of money in it,
Only binding round it.'

Perhaps there may be something in this, for within our recollection the 'gals and boys' of Massachusetts had something like it in their sports. But our version is a little different from the old lady's, and runs thus:—

'Lucy Locket lost her pocket
In a rainy shower;
Philip Carteret he ran arter it,
And found it in an hour.'

At a later period the Tories had a song commencing,—

'Yankee Doodle came to town
For to buy a firelock;
We will tar and feather him,
And so we will John Hancock.'

This version has a very strong resemblance to the original, the first line being the same, with the exception of the N for which the Y is substitued. The occurrence of the word 'feather' in the third line is no less remarkable. A long string of similar verses are known to exist, which were supposed to allude to the coming of Oliver Cromwell (on a small horse) into Oxford, with his single plume, which he wore fastened in a sort of knot, which the adherents of the royal party called 'a macaroni' out of derision. What renders the history of this tune the more remarkable is that to this very day the words of 'Lydia Locket,' alias 'Lucy Locket,' are sung to it by school children.

The tune is written in the same time, and has the same number of bars, as Yankee Doodle; and from its close resemblance, together with the identity of the words, we have little doubt but that the latter (Yankee Doodle) was composed as a sort of parody to the more ancient one; and though perhaps first used or adapted as a military air in 1755, as stated above, some other individual than Dr. Schackburg was the author."—Moore's Ency. of Music, Watson's Annals of Philadelphia.

"Some consider it an old vintage song of France; the Spaniards think their vales have echoed to its notes in early days; the following note is from a secretary of legation at Madrid:—   "Madrid, June 3, 1858.

My Dear Sir:—The tune 'Yankee Doodle,' from the first of my showing it here, has been acknowledged by persons acquainted with music to bear a strong resemblance to the popular airs of Biscay; and yesterday, a professor from the North recognized it as being much like the ancient sword dance played on solemn occasions by the people of San Sebastian. He says the tune varies in those provinces, and proposed in a couple of months to give me the changes as they are to be found in their different towns, that the matter may be judged of and fairly understood. Our national air certainly has its origin in the music of the free Pyrenees; the first strains are identically those of the heroic 'Danza Esparta,' as it was played to me, of brave old Biscay.   Very truly yours,   Buckingham Smith.

"The Magyars, with Louis Kossuth, recognize in it one of their old national dances. England entertains some shadowy tradition of its birth before the times of Cromwell; and the Dutchman claims it as a low country song of tithes and bonnyclabber; giving, it is said, as the original words:—

'Yanke dedel, doodel, down;
Dedel, dudel, lanter,
Yanke viner, vooner, vown,
Botermilk and tanther.'"—Extract from Nason's Monagram.

"That the air 'Yankee Doodle' was uniformly deemed a good retort on British royalists, we must be confirmed in, from the fact, that it was played by us at the battle of Lexington, when repelling the foe; again, at the surrender of Burgoyne; and, finally, at Yorktown surrender, when La Fayette, who ordered the tune, meant it as a retort on an intended affront."—Watson's Annals of Philadelphia.

*"When the British came out of the city to defile before us, we were ranged in two lines, the Americans on the right, and the French on the left; at the extremity of both lines were our general officers. In the midst of them, the beloved Washington was conspicuous, from his great height and beautiful charger, which he managed with inimitable grace. At the moment when the head of the column appeared, all eyes sought Cornwallis, who being detained by indisposition was represented by General O'Hara. The latter either through mistake or determination, offered his sword to General Rochambeau, who by a sign pointed out General Washington, and said that the French army being only auxiliary, it was from the American General that he should receive orders. O'Hara appeared piqued, and advanced towards Washington, who received him with a noble generosity. It was evident to us that the English in their misfortune were especially mortified to be obliged to lay down their arms before Americans, for the officers and soldiers affected to turn their heads towards the French line. Lafayette perceived this, and revenged himself in a very pleasant manner. He ordered the music of the light infantry to strike up 'Yankee Doodle,' an air which the British applied to a song composed to ridicule the Americans,—and which they uniformly sung to all their prisoners. This pleasantry of Lafayette was so bitter to them, that many of them broke their arms in a rage in grounding them on the glacis."—From "The Surrender of Cornwallis," in "Lafayette in America," by Levasseur.

APACHE INDIANS.

"Ma-Ma-Ma-Mine Ga-Ga."

SCALP SONG AND DANCE.

"While living near Tucson, Arizona, I saw the Apaches go through the ceremony of the Scalp-dance on several occasions. They place a pole in the centre of a *Plaza*, on the upper end of which is fastened a human scalp, decorated with colored ribbons, papers, etc. Around the base of the pole are squatted the squaws, who keep up the rhythm of the dance by rubbing with a corn-cob, a sort of *tom-tom*, made of clay baked in the sun and covered with skin. The *bucks* join hands and begin dancing in a circle, chanting the words, 'Ma-Ma-Ma-Mine Ga-Ga' to the above melody. After dancing in this manner for a short time, they go to another *plaza*, repeating the ceremony, changing again and again, until they are out of sight."—*Extract of letter, containing the above music, to the compiler, from Mr. Moses Katz, of Baltimore.*

ABYSSINIA.
TYPICAL SONGS.

"If the philosopher, in order to understand the genius of a nation, has need to study its manners and religion, and if a knowledge of its scientific works is necessary to the savant to appreciate its progress, it is equally necessary to gain a knowledge of the character of a people, to consider its poetry and music. These airs by their plaintive melody and rude pathos, give us a deep insight into the national character of the Abyssinians."—*Hotten's Abyssinia and its people.*

AFGHANISTAN.

Takhmi.

TYPICAL AIRS.

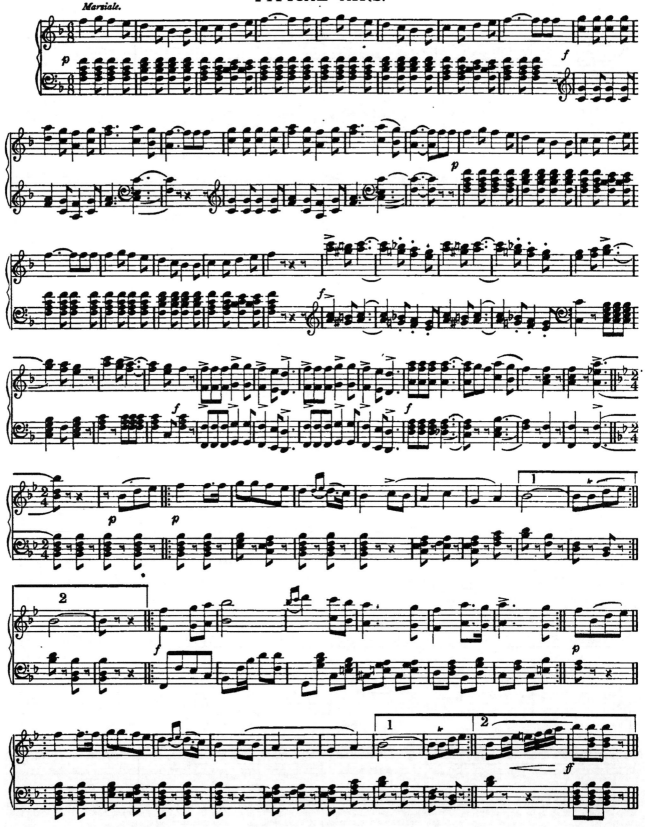

TYPICAL AIRS.

Arranged as a Quadrille by L. Luce, Director School of Singing of Algiers.

Salem, Salem.

Ye men K'ta Djebal.

" Except the Marseillaise, (the French hymn) there is no national song in Algeria. The natives (Arabs as well as Kabyles) sing, as a rule in solemn circumstances, verses of the Koran, and no notation exists of their religious airs. Among songs, the following are the most popular: *Salem, Salem, Ya men K'ta Djebal, El Dani thabou Kalbi, Ya tir en nouba, Dani Dan.* These have been arranged by Professor Luce, of Algiers, into a quadrille. This specimen will give quite an idea of the rhythm of the native music."-*Extract from despatch from the Consul of the United States at Algiers, Africa,* (1889).

El Dani ihabou Kalbi.

No. 3.

CODA.

Ya tir en nouba.

No. 4.

Dani! Dan!

ARABIA.

TYPICAL AIRS.

ARABIA.

SONG.

Song of the Bedouins.

ARGENTINE REPUBLIC.

Oid, mortales, el grito sagrado.

NATIONAL HYMM.

(25TH OF MAY, 1810.)

By Dr. Dn. Vincento Lopez.

ARGENTINE REPUBLIC.

Coro.

Sean eternos los laureles,
Que supimos conseguir;
Coronados de gloria vivamos,
O juremos con gloria morir.

1. Oid, mortales, el grito sagrado
Libertad, libertad, libertad,
Oid el ruido de rotas cadenas,
Ved en trono á la noble igualdad.
Se levanta á la faz de la tierra
Una nueva y gloriosa Nacion,
Coronada su sien de laureles,
Y á sus plantas rendido un leon.

Coro &a.

2. De los nuevos campeones los rostros
Marte mismo parece animar;
La grandeza se anida en sus pechos,
A su marcha todo hacen temblar.
Se conmueven del Inca las tumbas,
Y en sus huecos revive el ardor,
Lo que vé renovando á sus hijos
De la patria el antiguo esplendor.

Coro &a.

3. Pero, sierras y muros se sienten
Retumbar con horrible fragor;
Todo el pais se conturba por gritos
De venganza, de guerra y furor,
En los fieros tiranos la envidia
Escupió su pestífera hiel.
Su estandarte sangriento levantan,
Provocando á la lid mas cruel.

Coro &a.

4. ¿No los veis sobre Méjico y Quito
Arrojarse con zaña tenaz?
¿Y cuál lloran bañados en sangre
Potosi, Cochabamba y la Paz?
¿No los veis sobre el triste Caracas
Luto, llanto y muerte esparcir?
¿No los veis devorando cual fieras
Todo pueblo, que logran rendir?

Coro &a.

5. A vosotros se atreve, Argentinos,
El orgullo del vil invasor
Vuestros campos ya pisa contando,
Tantas glorias, hollar vencedor,
Mas los bravos, que unidos juraron
Su feliz libertad sostener,
A esos tigres sedientos de sangre
Fuertes pechos sabrán oponer.

Coro &a.

6. El valiente Argentino á las armas
Corre ardiendo con brio y valor;
El clarin de la guerra, cual trueno
En los campos del Sud resonó.
Buenos-Aires se pone á la frente
De los pueblos de la inclita Union,
Y con brazos robustos desgarran
Al Ibérico, altivo Leon.

Coro &a.

7. San Josè, San Lorenzo, Suipacha,
Ambas Piedras, Salta y Tucuman,
La Colonia y las mismas murallas,
Del tirano en la Banda Oriental,
Son letreros eternos, que dicen:
Aqui el brazo Argentino triunfó:
Aqui el fiero opresor de la patria
Su cerviz orgullosa dobló.

Coro &a.

8. La victoria al guerrero Argentino
Con sus alas brillantes cubrió,
Y azorado á su vista el tirano
Con infamia á la fuga se dió.
Sus banderas, sus armas se rinden
Por trofeos á la libertad,
Y sobre alas de gloria alza el pueblo
Trono digno á su gran magestad.

Coro &c.

9. Desde un polo hasta el otro resuena
De la fama el sonoro clarin,
Y de América el nombre enseñando
Les repite—mortales oid? . . . .
Ya su trono dignisimo abrieron
Las Provincias unidas del Sud
Y los libres del mundo responden:
Al gran pueblo Argentino, Salud!

Coro &a.

ARMENIA.

Nor Oghchioon.　(Glad Tidings.)

PATRIOTIC SONG.

By Bishop Minas.

Glad tid - ings, oh, Ar - me - nian bards we bring, Our hills and vales with

shouts of freedom ring; In hum - ble-ness our Sav-iour we in-voke, To o - vèr-throw the cru - el Turk-ish yoke. So

tune your harps for free - dom, Strike the chords of gold, Sing Ar - me - nia's prais - es As in days of old, So

tune your harps for free - dom, Strike the chords of gold, Sing Ar - me - nia's prais - es As in days of old.

The compiler secured the above song through hearing it sung by an Armenian gentleman, now (1889) in the United States. This gentleman states that about two years since, the Turkish Government ordered its officers to destroy whenever found all Armenian patriotic music, poetry and paintings. The order has been so zealously obeyed that little remains of Armenia's history in song and story.

AUSTRALIA
The Song of Australia.
PATRIOTIC SONG.

Words by Mrs. C. J. Carleton.

Music by Carl Linger.

1. There is a land where summer skies Are gleaming with a thousand dyes, Blending in witching harmonies, in harmonies And grassy knoll and forest height Are flushing in the rosy light, And all above is azure bright Australia, Australia, Australia!

2. There is a land where honey flows, Where laughing corn luxuriant grows; Land of the myrtle and the rose, myrtle and rose. On hill and plain the clus'tring vine Is gushing out with purple wine; And cups are quaff'd to thee and thine, Australia, Australia, Australia!

3. There is a land where treasures shine Deep in the dark unfathom'd mine For worshippers at Mammon's shrine, at Mammon's shrine; Where gold lies hid, and rubies gleam, And fabl'd wealth no more doth seem The idle fancy of a dream, Australia, Australia, Australia!

4.
There is a land where homesteads peep
From sunny plain and woodland steep,
And love and joy bright vigils keep;
Where the glad voice of childish glee
Is mingling with the melody
Of nature's hidden minstrelsy.
Australia!

5.
There is a land where, floating free,
From mountain top to girdling sea,
A proud flag waves exultingly;
And freedom's sons the banner bear;
No shackl'd slave can breathe the air—
Fairest of Britain's daughters fair,
Australia!

"The history of this composition is as follows: Some twenty or twenty-five years ago the committee of the Mechanics' Institute in Gawler, South Australia, offered a prize of 25gs for the best Australian ode, to be called the national song of Australia. There was a great deal of competition; and eventually the prize was awarded to Mrs. C. J. Carleton, of Adelaide. The committee next offered a prize for the most appropriate music for these words; and, after another competition, the composition of Herr Carl Linger, at that time the leading professional musician in the colony, and a quiet, thorough-going scientific man, was accepted. When his air, composed to Mrs. Carleton's words, was published, it at once took the popular taste in South Australia—the people there were exceedingly critical in musical matters then—and it has since held full possession of South Australians. Next to the National Anthem it is the air which is played at all public gatherings, hummed in every home, and fully recognised as the hymn of the people."-*From the Town and Country Journal, New South Wales.*

AUSTRIA.

God preserve our noble Emperor.
NATIONAL HYMN.

Words by Laurence Leopold Haschka, (1797.)

Music by J. Haydn (1797).

3.
To array himself in virtue,
 Ever was his constant care;
Only to defend his people
 Doth his sword flame high in air.
In their blessings thus rewarded,
 He finds all his pleasure there.
God preserve our noble Emp'ror,
Franz our Emp'ror good and great!

4.
Bonds of slav'ry he hath broken,
 He has made his people free;
He of knighthood is the flower,
 Brave and good and true is he;
And when comes his latest hour,
 May he by angels greeted be.
God preserve our noble Emp'ror,
Franz our Emp'ror good and great!

3.
Sich mit Tugenden zu schmücken,
 Achtet er der Sorgen werth.
Nicht, um Völker zu erdrücken,
 Flammt in seiner Hand das Schwert;
Sie zu segnen, zu beglücken,
 Ist der Preis, den er begehrt.
Gott erhalte Frans den Kaiser,
Unsern guten Kaiser Frans!

4.
Er zerbrach der Knechtschaft Bande,
 Hob zur Freiheit uns empor!
Früh erleb' er deutscher Lande,
 Deutscher Völker höchsten Flor
Und vernehme noch am Rande
 Später Gruft der Enkel Chor:
Gott erhalte Frans den Kaiser,
Unsern guten Kaiser Frans!

When Haydn visited England, he was so much interested in the effect of "God Save the King" on the public on solemn occasions, he resolved, after his return to Vienna, to present his own country with a similar composition. Haydn's friend, Freiherr von Swieten, suggested the idea to the Prime Minister, Graf von Saurau, and the poet Haschka was commissioned to write the words which Haydn set in January, 1797. On the Emperor's birthday, Feb. 12th, the air was sung simultaneously at the National theatre in Vienna and at all the principal theatres in the provinces.—*Engel, et al.*

AUSTRIA.

Oh! thou my Austria!

PATRIOTIC SONG.

Music by F. von Suppé, born April 18, 1820.

1. Where snow-crown'd mountains rear their sum - mits
2. Yes, there, where Al - pine maids the gay - est

t'wards the sky, As tho' they con - verse held with clouds in Heav'n on high.
dit - ties sing, Where youths the sweet - est flow'rs to blush - ing maid - ens bring.

Where pure from
Where ech - oes

sparkling springs flow wa - ters crys - tal clear, Where cha - mois fleet are chas'd by youths who ne'er know fear, Who aim, when
far and near ring clear - ly on the air, Where faith and love go hand and hand in un - ion fair, Ah! there where

far a - bove on rock - y steep they stand, Who aim, when far a - bove on rock - y steep they stand; } Yes, that is my Aus - tri - a!
faith and love go ev - er hand in hand, Ah! there where faith and love go ev - er hand in hand;

That is my Fa-ther-land! That is my Aus-tri-a! My Fa-ther-land!

CARNIOLA.

My home to the East by Croatia is bounded.

TYPICAL SONG.

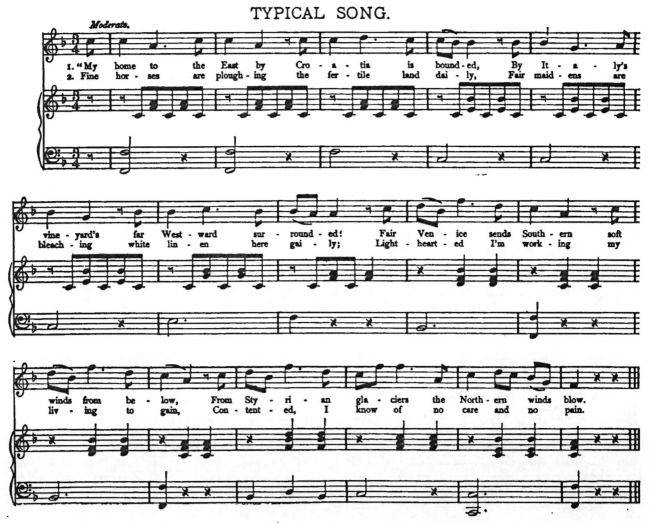

1. "My home to the East by Cro-a-tia is bound-ed, By It-a-ly's
2. Fine hor-ses are plough-ing the fer-tile land dai-ly, Fair maid-ens are

vine-yard's far West-ward sur-round-ed! Fair Ven-ice sends South-ern soft
bleach-ing white lin-en here gai-ly; Light-heart-ed I'm work-ing my

winds from be-low, From Sty-ri-an gla-ciers the North-ern winds blow.
liv-ing to gain, Con-tent-ed, I know of no care and no pain.

BELGIUM.

La Brabanconne.

NATIONAL AIR:

By F. Campenhout.

BENGAL.

Kutch Kewhana.

NAUTCH AIR.

BERAR.

AN AIR OF THE DECCAN.

BERAR.

BOHEMIA.

War-song of the Hussites.

NATIONAL SONG.

(About 1460.)

In the Overture to "The Bohemian Girl" Balfe has used this melody as the principal motive of the Allegro.

BOLIVIA.

Bolivia nos el ha.

NATIONAL AIR:

By De Benedicto Vincentti.

BOLIVIA.

BULGARIA

Maritza.

NATIONAL AIR.

BOSNIA.

Mountains bath'd in morning light.

TYPICAL SONG.

1. Mountains bath'd in morn-ing light, Lark's sweet lays to work in-vite. Come my flocks to flow-'ry mead,
2. Maid, than sun-light bright-er far, Fair-er than the morn-ing star; Lips of hon-ey, cheeks of rose,

Shall your lov-ing shep-herd lead, Come my flocks to flow-'ry mead, Shall your lov-ing shep-herd lead.
Fare-ye-well till daylight's close! Lips of hon-ey, cheeks of rose, Fare-ye-well till daylight's close!

BURMAH.

(Kayah Than.) Sound the Trumpet.
NATIONAL AIR:

BURMAH.

CANADA.

The Maple Leaf Forever.

PATRIOTIC SONG

Composed by ALEXANDER MUIR.

1. In days of yore, from Bri-tain's shore, Wolfe the daunt-less he-ro came, And plant-ed firm Bri-tan-nia's flag, On Ca-na-da's fair do-main! Here may it wave, our boast, our pride, And joined in love to-

2. At Queens-ton Heights, and Lun-dy's Lane, Our brave fa-ther's side by side, For free-dom, homes, and loved ones dear, Firm-ly stood, and no-bly died; And those dear rights which they main-tained, We swear to yield them

3. Our fair Do-min-ion now ex-tends From Cape Race to Noot-ka Sound; May peace for-ev-er be our lot, And plen-te-ous store a-bound; And may those ties of love be ours Which dis-cord can-not

4. On Mer-ry Eng-land's far famed land May kind Heav-en sweet-ly smile; God bless Old Scot-land ev-er-more, And Ire-land's Em-er-ald Isle! Then swell the song, both loud and long, Till rocks and for-est

"This air is the favorite in Western Canada, with the English speaking Canadians, though it is well-known all over the Dominion. "God Save the Queen" is the only official national air, and is played on all occasions of ceremony, especially at the conclusion of any performance, ball or fete."—*Extract from Despatch from Hon. Richard G. Lay, Consul-General at Ottawa.*

CANADA.

CANADA.

Vive la Canadienne.

TYPICAL SONG OF THE FRENCH-CANADIANS.

L. STREABBOG.

This air is more especially the favorite with the French speaking Canadians and is best known in the Lower Provinces.

Vive la Canadienne.

I.

Vive la Canadienne,
　Soar, my heart, oh soar,
Vive la Canadienne,
‖: How beauteous are her eyes. :‖

2.

The wedding bells are calling her,
　Soar, my heart, oh soar,
The wedding bells are calling her,
‖: She's dressed in grand attire. :‖

3.

We're dancing with our pretty blondes,
　Soar, my heart, oh soar,
We're dancing with our pretty blondes,
‖: We're changing step by step. :‖

4.

We'll pass the brimming flagon round,
　Soar, my heart, oh soar,
We'll pass the brimming flagon round,
‖: And take a drink to cheer. :‖

5.

Our happiness increases,
　Soar, my heart, oh soar,
Our happiness increases,
‖: The wine cup we adore. :‖

I.

Vive la Canadienne,
　Vole, mon cœur, vole,
Vive la Canadienne,
　Et ses jolis yeux doux,
Et ses jolis yeux doux, doux, doux,
　Et ses jolis yeux doux.

2.

Nous la menons aux noces,
　Vole, mon cœur, vole,
Nous la menons aux noces,
　Dans tous ses beaux atours. (Ter.)

3.

On danse avec nos blondes,
　Vole, mon cœur, vole,
On danse avec nos blondes;
　Nous changeons tour à tour. (Ter.)

4.

On passe la carafe,
　Vole, mon cœur, vole,
On passe la carafe;
　Nous buvons tous un coup. (Ter.)

5.

Mais le bonheur augmente,
　Vole, mon cœur, vole,
Mais le bonheur augmente,
　Quand nous sommes tous soûls. (Ter.)

CELEBES ISLANDS.

AIR.

CAPE VERD ISLANDS.

Lundum.
NATIVE DANCE

Trenéné.
TYPICAL AIR.

Cha Bai. (Let us go.)
AIR OF THE ISLAND OF BOA VISTA.

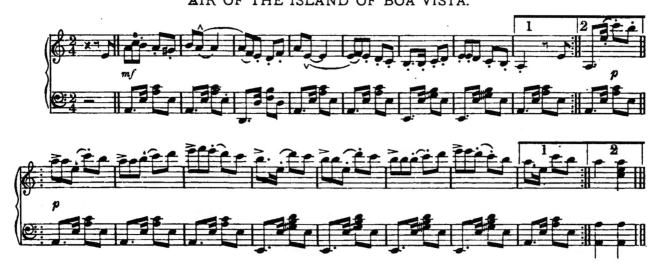

CAPE VERD ISLANDS.

Cheraben. (Sweet smell.)

AIR OF BRAVA ISLANDS.

Manche.

AIR OF THE ISLAND OF FOGO.

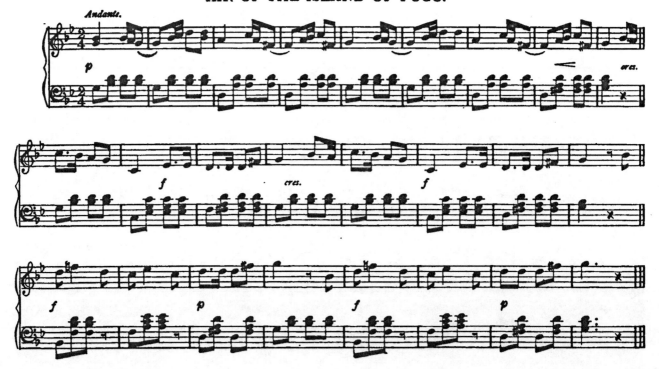

CARINTHIA.

Our Valley.

TYPICAL SONG.

In Kla-gen-furt's fair val-ley Where the limpid wa-ters flow, Lives a maid to whom I'm grateful, If e'en greeting she'll be-stow. In Ro-sen-thal the maidens Are fair I've heard them tell, From the bound'ry of Saint Jo-seph, To the ve-ry end of Zell!

CASHMERE.

TYPICAL AIR:

CASHMERE.

CHEROKEE INDIANS.

Híganúyahí.
BALL SONGS.

Yo wi Danuwe Yowida-Danuwe.

Prof. James Mooney of the Bureau of Ethnology, who sang the above airs for the compiler, has spent several years among the Cherokees. In speaking of their music, he says: "As Cherokee songs are always in the minor key they have a plaintive effect, even when the sentiment is cheerful or even boisterous and calculated to excite the mirth of one who understands the language. This impression is heightened by the appearance of the dancers themselves, for the women shuffle solemnly back and forth all night long without ever a smile upon their faces, while the occasional laughter of the men seems half subdued, with none of the hearty, ringing tones of the white man or negro. The monotonous repetition, too, is something intolerable to any one but an Indian, the same words to the same tune being sometimes sung over and over again for a half hour or more. Although the singer improvises as he proceeds, many of the expressions have now become stereotyped, and are used at almost every ball play dance. The songs here given are good types of the ball songs and were heard on several occasions.

The words have no fixed order of arrangement and may be strung out indefinitely. Higanuyahi is the refrain sung by the women and has no meaning. The vowels have the Latin sound and 'u' is the French nasal 'un':—

Higanúya, higanúyahi
Higanúya, higanúyahi
Sákwili-téga tsitûkatásûni!
Astalitiaki tsitûkatásûni!
Astalitiaki tsákwakilûtesti!
Uwatûhi tsitûkatásûni!
Tikananéhi ákwakilûtati!
Uwátutsûhi tsákwakilûtati!
Uwátutsûhi tsitûkatásûni!
Igeakiyu tsákwakilûtesti!
Tikananéhi tsitûkatásûni!—Hu!

But sic transit gloria—in these degenerate days the pacer is more apt to be a jack knife."

Which may be freely rendered:—
What a fine horse I shall win!
I shall win a pacer!
I shall be riding a pacer.
I'm going to win a pretty one!
A stallion for me to ride!
What a pretty one I shall win!
What a pretty one I shall ride!
How proud I'll feel when riding him!
I'm going to win a stallion!—Hu!

CHIPPEWA INDIANS.
SCALP DANCE.

CHILI.

Dulce Patria.

NATIONAL AIR.

Composed by Carnicer.

CHILI.

The Cueca.

NATIONAL DANCE:

CHINA.

"The World's Delight."

NATIONAL AIR.

64

CHINA.

Moo-lee-wha.

FLOWER SONG.

COSTA-RICA.
De la Patria.
NATIONAL SONG:

By Mel. Ma. Gutierrez.

1. With a love for our glorious nation,
   And the fame that enshrines her in story,
   With a patriot's true inspiration,
   We will sing of her deeds and her glory.

2. Let our voices be clear and resounding,
   From the Andes across to the ocean;
   Let the mountains and valleys surrounding,
   Loudly echo our hymn of devotion!

3. From the forests and gardens of flowers,
   Let the echo be fervent and ringing,
   While with love to the altar of Freedom
   We our pledges of honor are bringing. *Translation by E. M. T.*

1. De la pátria el azur nos inspira,
   Eleitucos le un himno triumfal,
   De Tirteo, eu la bélica lira!
   Celebrêneos su gloria iu mortal.

2. Nuestra vos acordada resuene viril,
   Desde el Ande gigante á la uear!
   Y repitan los valles cual eco rugiente,
   Las fervidas notas del patrio cautar.

3. Desde el bosque sombrio al florida vergel
   Cuuda el eco, potente, sublime, ferviente,
   Y al ara beudita, holocausto de azur,
   Las pre ces lleveucos de gloria y honor.

CROATIA.

Hrvatska Domovina.

NATIONAL SONG.

Nek se hrusti.

TYPICAL SONG.

CUBA.

La Bayamesa.

SONG OF THE GUARACHAS.

1. Dost re-mem-ber, oh maid-en of Ba-ya-mo, That my sun was the brightness of your

1. *No te a cuer-das gen-til Ba-ya-me-sa que tu fuis-te mi sol re-ful*

"Cuba, being a province and dependency of Spain, has no national air of her own. During the insurrection of some years ago, several songs obtained ephemeral popularity, on account of supposed allusions to the political situation, but are now no longer heard.

The 'Zapateo Cubano,' however, may be considered as the essentially popular Cuban air, as it is the favorite one of the 'Gaujairos,' or Cuban countrymen. It is sung in high falsetto voice, often in part to the accompaniment of the 'Tiple,' a kind of small Mandolin, and the patting of hands, while a couple may be engaged in dancing, and keeping time to the music, in a series of short, shuffling steps. The words, generally in praise of country life, love, etc., are often improvisations.

'La Bayemesa' is an old and popular air. 'The Guaracha' is a song popular among the colored people, especially of Havana."—*From the Hon. Joseph A. Springer Vice-Consul General at Havana*

CUBA.

love - lit eyes,— How I joy - ful - ly kissed your brow of beau - ty While you gazed at me with a sweet sur -
gen - - te cuando ale - green tu cán-di-da frèn-te blan-do be-zo im-pri-mi con ar-

prise? Dost re - mem - ber, love, when words of soft-ness thrilled......... me, When your heart so pure was mine but to a -
dor, no re-cuer - das queun ti-em-po di-cho - - so me es - ta-sie con tu pu - ra be-

dore?....................... No cru - el words of dark-some doubt had chilled me, For we
ile - - za y do-blan - do los dos la ca-be - za o-fre-

prom - ised to be true for ev - er - more.
ci - mos a-mar - nos los dos.

2.

At your window, my darling, I am singing,—
  Come awake, gaze at him whose heart is filled with grief!—
Ope thy lattice, my darling, to my pleading,
  And with love give my aching heart relief.
Oh recall, my darling, days of joy and gladness,
  When sweet love was our only thought by day or night.
Let us banish all thoughts of grief and sadness,
  And to love bow with unrestrained delight.

2.

A mi canto despierta sonriendo,
Ven y mírame al pié de tus rejas;
Ven, no duermas y atiende á mis quejas,
Pon remedio o mi negro dolor;
  Recordando las glorias pasadas
Disipemos, mi bien, la tristeza,
Y doblando los dos la cabeza
Morirémos de gusto y amor.

CUBA.

Zapateo Cubano.

TYPICAL SONG.

By Gabriel Vilá.

Canto.

1. Morn - ing so ro - sy and beau - ti - ful, Will soon make its ap - pear - ance.—
2. Silk cot - ton trees of A - mer - i - ca Will rear their heads so proud - ly;

1. Pron - to ven - drá la ma - na - na, en que la ne - bli - na den - sa,—
2. Las cei - bas a - me - ri - ca - nas, seal - sa - rán so - bre los mon - tes,

Canto.

Morn - ing so ro - sy and beau - ti - ful, Will soon make its ap - pear - ance; Then the mist will rise re -
Mu - sic me - lo - dious the birds will trill, While in the sky the sun so bright, Will shine up - on the

Pron - to ven - drá la ma - na - na, en que la ne - bli - na den - sa, ex - tien - da su ca - pain -
Les me - lo - dio - sos sin - son - tes tri - na - rán a - qui ya - llá y el sol iu - lu - mi - na -

CUBA.

CUBA.

La Territorial.

TYPICAL AIR.

M. Saumell.

Con 8va abajo..

CUBA.

El Mondonguito.
TYPICAL AIR.

By R. Valenzuela.

"El Mondonguito' means 'tripe.' The melody was first sung in the streets of Havana, by a vender of that commodity; it became immensely popular and is one of the best known Cuban airs."

DALECARLIA.

Brave of heart and warriors bold.

PATRIOTIC SONG.

1. Brave of heart and war-riors bold, Were the Swedes from time un-told;
2. Song of many a thou-sand year, Rings thro' wood and val-ley clear;

Breasts for hon-or ev-er warm, Youth-ful strength in he-ro arm!
Pic-ture thou of wa-ters wild, Yet as tears of mourn-ing mild.

Blue eyes bright Dance with light, For thy dear green val-leys old;
To the rhyme Of past time, Blend all hearts and lists each ear.

North! thou gi-ant limb of earth, With thy friend-ly, home-ly hearth!
Guard the songs of Swe-dish lore, Love and sing them ev-er-more.

DENMARK.

King Christian stood beside the mast.

NATIONAL SONG.

Words by EWALD.

Music by HARTMAN.

This song was introduced in an Operetta, "The Fisherman," composed by Johann Hartman, and became very popular throughout Denmark. Hartman was a German, who settled in Copenhagen in 1768, where he died in 1791.—*Engel*.

no man can, The pow'r of Den - mark's Chris - ti - an, The pow'r of
fyj te can! Hvo staar for Dan - marks Kris - ti - an, Hvo staar for

Den - mark's Chris - ti - an Re - sist!
Dan - marks Kris - ti - en I Kamp!

2.

Nils Juel gave heed to the tempest's roar,
  Now is the hour!
He hoisted his blood-red flag once more,
And smote upon the foe full sore,
And shouted loud through the tempest's roar,
  "Now is the hour!"
"Fly," shouted they, "for shelter fly!
Of Denmark's Juel who can defy
  The power?"

3.

North Sea! a glimpse of Wessel rent
  Thy murky sky!
Then champions to thine arms were sent;
Terror and death glared where he went;
From the waves was heard a wail that rent
  Thy murky sky!
From Denmark thunders Thordenskiold,
Let each to heaven commend his soul
  And fly!

4.

Path of the Dane to fame and might!
  Dark rolling wave!
Receive thy friend who, scorning flight,
Goes to meet danger with despite—
Proudly as thou the tempest's might,
  Dark rolling wave!
And 'midst thy pleasures and alarms,
And war and victory, be thine arms
  My grave!

2.

Nils Juel gav Agt paa Stormens Brag,
  Nu er det Tid!
Han hejsede det rode Flag
Og slog paa Fjenden Slag i Slag.
Da skreg de hojt blandt Stormens Brag:
  "Nu er del Tid!"
"Fly," skreg de, "hver som vid et Skjul!
Hvo kan bestaa for Danmarks Juel
  I Strid!"

3.

O Nordhav, Glimt af Vessel brod
  Din morke Sky!
Da lyde Kamper til dit Skjod,
Thi med ham lynte Skrak og Dod.
Fra Vallen hortes Vraal, som brod
  Den tykke Sky.
Fra Danmark lyner Tordenskjold;
Hver giv sig i Himlens Vold
  Og fly!

4.

Du danskes Vej ti Ros og Magt,
  Sortladne Hav!
Modtag din Ven, som uforsagt
Vor mode Faren med Foragt,
Saa stolt som du mod Stormens Magt,
  Sortlande Hav!
Og rask igjennem Larm og Spil
Og Kamp og Sejer for mig til
  Min Grav.

DENMARK.

The Dannebrog.
PATRIOTIC SONG:

By Bay.

4.
As stars in heav'n, so many,
   Great warriors thou canst name;
Yet of them all, not any
   Eclipse our Christian's fame;
He, armour-clad, victorious,
   Sees from the shores of light
How oft a hero glorious
   Appears for Denmark's right.

5.
See, Christian's palm appearing,
   Whene'er thy cross, pure white,
Its crest is proudly rearing
   To spur the Danes in fight;
On every wind be flying,
   Thy sons all cherish thee,
Thy fame will be undying
   Till waves shall vanish'd be!

6.
On Dana's shore wave proudly,
   Fly high on Indian land;
Hark! as the waves beat loudly
   On Barb'ry's far-off strand,
Thy praises they are singing,
   And of thy knights so dear,
High t'wards Walhalla ringing,
   Where heroes pause to hear.

7.
See those to thee remaining,
   Glow as thy purple red;
For thee, by love unwaning,
   To death and vict'ry led.
O thou, our glory's token,
   Float high on every shore,
Till northern armor's broken,
   And Danes' heart beat no more!

"Prompted by Pope Gregory IX, King Valdemar the Conqueror undertook an expedition to Esthonia for the purpose of converting the heathen there to christianity, 1219. The Danes were almost defeated, when, (as states the legend,) the *Dannebrog*-banner fell from heaven, and raised them to victory. This saying undoubtedly arose from the fact that the Pope gave Valdemar for this undertaking a "holy banner,"—blood red, with a white cross in the centre—which became later the Danes' chief standard in all their wars, till it was lost to them in the unfortunate expedition to Ditmarsh in 1500."—*Songs of Northern Europe.*

DENMARK.

Towards the North.
PATRIOTIC SONG.

C. F. Weyse.

4.
Far southward where the Elbe's soft waves are playing,
  Where thousand ships rock near the verdant strand;
'Midst many golden sheaves the kine are straying,
  And graze contented on the fertile land.
Where in the Baltic storm-birds wild are crying,
  Stands Bornholm's mighty breast on Rocky ground,
Deep in its heart are sparkling treasures lying,
  And men there laugh aloud at danger's sound.

5.
Thus stream and Sound the towns and meadows sever,
  Yet Denmark stands united in its might,
A nation's faithful love will bind it ever,
  And honor stands a guardian for its right.
A common cause here every heart is blending,
  And loving children guard each native shore,
All Danish hearts one pray'r to Heav'n are sending,
  God guard our king and land for evermore.

DENMARK.

Denmark, by whose verdant strand.

PATRIOTIC SONG.

R. Bay.

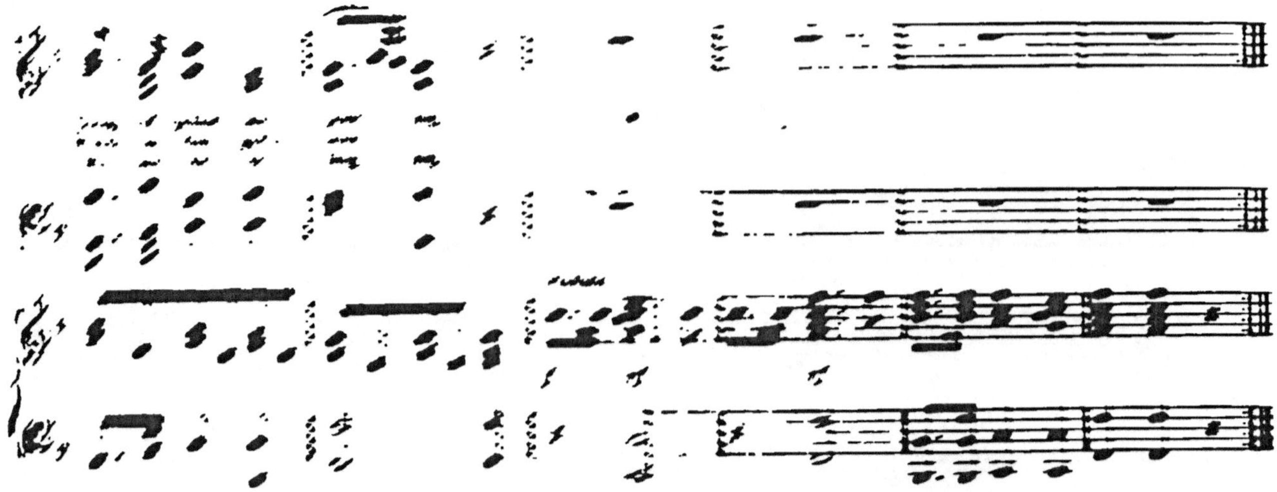

4

[illegible]

5

Let our songs ring clear and high,
[illegible]
We'll together live and die,
True in death remaining!
Brothers, let us all here aid
Denmark's fame to nourish;
Long live king, and land, and maid,
Long may Denmark flourish!

Chorus (ad lib.)—Brothers, let us all here aid
Denmark's fame to nourish;
Long live king, and land, and maid,
Long may Denmark flourish!

DENMARK.

A Soldier Brave.

PATRIOTIC SONG.

HORNEMANN.

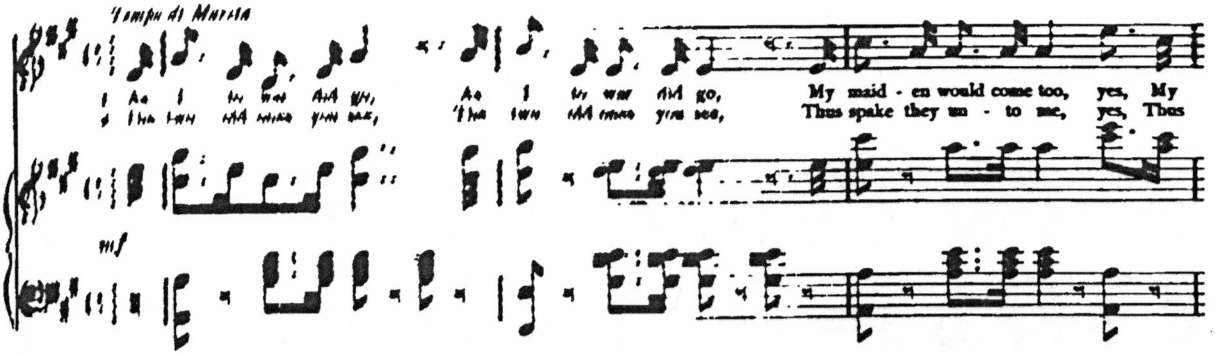

if   no ball does hit   me, why, Soon home a - gain I'll rove.   Ah! were the foe not near,......   I
who will plough for us our fields, And who the grass will mow?" Yes, that is just the rea - son why

ne'er   to war would go;   Yet all the Dan - ish maid - ens now count on me, you know,   And
we   must march, hur - rah!   Or else will come the Ger - mans* and help us from a - far;   And

there - fore I'll fight brave - ly,   as val - iant sol - dier true!   Hur - rah! hur - rah! hur - rah!
there - fore I'll fight brave - ly,   as val - iant sol - dier true!   Hur - rah! hur - rah! hur - rah!

3. ‖: If now the Germans near, :‖
   I pity all men here, yes,
   I pity all men here;
   To Peter and to Paul,
   They say: "you're lazy all;"
And if one scold in Danish, why, " Holls maul!"† they loudly call!
If one could but in words, ah! upon them vengeance wreak!
Yet there are far too many who only Danish speak.
And therefore I'll fight bravely, as valiant soldier true!
   Hurrah! hurrah! hurrah!

4. ‖: The Dannebrog know I, :‖
   It fell from heaven high, yes,
   It fell from heaven high;
   It waves upon the sea,
   Before the people free;
You'll never find a banner which could like unto it be!
And they have mocked its glory with deeds profane and bold.
Ha! thereunto our banner is far too good and old!
And therefore I'll fight bravely, as valiant soldier true!
   Hurrah! hurrah! hurrah!

5. ‖: Why should we fear the foe? :‖
   Our king's our friend, we know, yes,
   Our king's our friend, we know,
   He bears a shining sword,
   He strikes and wastes no word;
And always 'fore a Danish king one is a little awed.
Yet now they all behave as tho' he no more were free!
Ha! much they like to have him in German slavery!
And therefore I'll fight bravely, as valiant soldier true!
   Hurrah! hurrah! hurrah!

6. ‖:For maiden and for land, :‖
   We all will take our stand, yes,
   We all will take our stand,
   And shame on those who slight
   Their language true and right,
And do not for the Dannebrog storm onward to the fight.
Ah! should I ne'er come back here to greet the homestead dear,
I'm sure my king will comfort for me my old ones here!
And therefore I'll fight bravely, as valiant soldier true!
   Hurrah! hurrah! hurrah!

* German-Danish war, regarding the annexation of Schleswig-Holstein to Prussia.   † North German dialect for "shut up!"

EAST INDIA.

TYPICAL AIRS.

THOWRANI ROOP. Manipuri Air.

Burmese Air.

EAST INDIA.
The Gazelle.
SONG.

EGYPT.

Salaam Effindina; or, Khedival March.

NATIONAL AIR.

ECUADOR.

Salve, oh Patria.

NATIONAL SONG.

Translation by J. H. Thomas
Versification by Edward M. Taber.

We sa-lute thee, and praise thee, our na - - tion, Hail, all hail, Hail, all
Salve, oh Pa - tria, mil ve - ces! oh Pa - - tria, gloria a ti gloria a

Hail all hail!
gloria a ti,

hail! To the land of our hearts ad-o-ra - tion, To the land of our hearts ad-o-ra - tion.
ti, ya en tu pe cho en tu pe cho re bo - sa gora y par en tu pe cho re bo - sa.

hail, all hail!
gloria a ti,

Joy and peace fill thy great heart for-ev - - er, Till thy life blood no long-er shall
y tu fren-te y tu fren-te ra-dio - sa masque el sol con-tem-pla-mos lu-

run,............... For the star in thy fore-head is bright — er Than the light of the trop - i - cal
cir,............... y tu frente, y tu fren - te ra - dio - sa masque el sol con - tem - pla - mos lu

sun. Joy and sun. Filled with righteous and fierce in - dig - na - tion, At the
cir. y tu cir. In - dig - na - dos tus hi - jos del yu - go que kim

yoke of a deep deg - ra - da - tion, Laid by in - so - lent Spain on our na - tion, Thy brave sons raised their voice to thy
pu - so la i - berica an - da - cia, de la in - jus - ta y horrend a des - gra - cia que pe - sa - ba fatal so - bre

ESKIMO INDIANS.

SONGS.

Summer Song.

The Returning Hunter.

Song of the Tornit.

" Among the arts of the Eskimo, poetry and music are by far the most prominent. * * 'The Summer Song' and 'The Returning Hunter' may be most frequently heard. As to the contents of the songs, they treat of almost anything imaginable :—of the beauty of summer; of thought and feelings of the composer on any occasion, for instance, when watching a seal, when angry with somebody, etc.; or they tell of an important event, as of a long journey."—*The Central Eskimo, by Dr. Franz Boas.*

FAYAL.
NATIONAL AIR.
(Composed in 1821.)

By Wm. Searle.

FIJI ISLANDS.

Autiko mai na.

AIR.

Free translation:—I was sleeping in the Tamba-tangane,
A red cock crowed near the house,
I woke up suddenly and cried,
I was going to get some Kundravi flowers,
For a wreath in the harmonious dance.

"The music of the Fiji Islands is more rude than of any people we have had communication with in the South Seas. The men rarely care for music, nor have they any pleasure in musical sounds. The tones of the violin, accordion, flute and musical-box, which caused so much delight among other islanders, had no charms for them. Their attention is seldom riveted by these instruments, and they will walk off insensible to the sweetest notes."—*Narrative of the U. S. Exploring Expedition by Charles Wilkes, U. S. N.*

FINLAND.

Our land. (Vart land.)
NATIONAL SONG.

Words by J. L. Runeberg.

Music by F. Pacius.

2.

Our land is poor as all can tell;
  No gold our rivers hold;
A stranger scorns its heath and fell;
And yet this land we love full well;
  For us—with mountain wood and wold—
  'Tis still a land of gold.

3.

We love our rivers thundering tide,
  Our streamlets sparkling bright;
The murmuring of our forests wide,
Our starry nights, our summer's pride,
  All, all that e'er, with sound or sight,
  Has filled us with delight.

4.

'Twas here our fathers fought the fight
  With thoughts and sword and plough;
Here, here in moments dark or bright,
'Mid fortune's smile, or fortune's spite,
  The Finnish people's heart would glow,
  'Twould bear both weal and woe.

5.

And who could count the struggles dire
  Which that brave people stood,
When battle raged with sword or fire,
And frost and famine spent their ire;
  And who could meet their outspread blood,
  Their patient, dauntless mood?

6.

It was for us their life-blood flowed,
  Here, here, upon this shore;
'Twas here with joy their bosoms glowed;
'Twas here in sorrow they abode:
  Long ere we lived, in days of yore,
  Our burdens here they bore.

7.

How blest, how precious is this spot,
  All that we love is here,
Howe'er hard fate may cast our lot,
A land, a fatherland—we've got;
  Oh, what on earth can fairly e'er
  Be to our hearts more dear?

8.

And here, aye here we see this land,
  Oh sight, how full of bliss!
We need but stretch the lifted hand,
And joyous point to sea and strand,
  And say: Behold! this country—this—
  Our fatherland it is!

9.

And were we called to dwell in light,
  'Midst golden clouds of morn,
Where thousand stars are glittering bright,
Where tears ne'er flow, nor sorrows blight;
  Still for this land so poor, so stern,
  Our longing soul would yearn.

10.

Oh land! thou land of thousand lakes,
  Of song and constancy,
Against whose strand life's ocean breaks,
Where dreams the past; the future wakes;
  Oh! blush not for thy poverty,
  Be hopeful, bold and free!

11.

Thy blossom in the bud that lies
  Shall burst its fetters strong;
Lo! from our tender love shall rise
Thy light, thy fame, thy hopes, thy joys;
  And prouder far shall sound ere long
  Our Finland's patriot song!

2.

Vårt länd är fattigt, skall så blå
  För den, som guld begär;
En främling far oss stolt förbi,
Men detta landet älska vi,
  För oss med moar, fjäll och skär
  Ett guldland dock det är.

3.

Vi älska våra strömmars brus
  Och våra backars språng,
Den mörka skogens dystra sus,
Vår stjernenatt, vårt sommarljus,
  Allt, allt, hvad här som syn, som sång
  Vårt hjerta rört en gång.

4.

Här strìddes våra fäders strid
  Med tanke, svärd och plog,
Här, här, i klar som mulen tid,
Med lycka hård, med lycka blid,
  Det Finska folkets hjerta slog,
  Här bars hvad det fördrog.

5.

Hvem täljde väl de striders tal,
  Som detta folk bestod,
Då kriget röt från dal till dal,
Då frosten kom med hungrens qval,
  Hvem mätte allt dess spillda blod,
  Och allt dess tålamod?

6.

Och det var här, det blodet flöt,
  Ja här för oss det var,
Och det var här sin fröjd det njöt,
Och det var här sin suck det göt,
  Det folk, som våra bördor bar
  Långt före våra dar.

7.

Här är oss ljuft, här är oss godt,
  Här är oss allt beskärdt;
Huru ödet kastar än vår lott,
Ett länd, ett fosterland vi fått,
  Hvad finns på jorden mera värdt
  Att hållas dyrt och kärt?

8.

Och här och här är detta land,
  Vårt öga ser det här;
Vi kunna sträcka ut vår hand,
Och visa gladt på sjö och strand
  Och säga: se! det landet der,
  Vårt fosterland det är!

9.

Och fördes vi att bo i glans
  Bland guldmoln i det blå,
Och blef vårt lif en stjernedans,
Der tår ej göts, der suck ej fanns,
  Till detta arma land ändå
  Vår längtan skulle stå.

10.

O land, du tusen sjöars land,
  Der sång och trohet byggt,
Der lifvets haf oss gett en strand,
Vår forntids land, vår framtids land,
  Var för din fattigdom ej skyggt,
  Var fritt, var gladt, var tryggt.

11.

Din blomning, sluten än i knopp
  Skall mogna ur sitt tvång;
Se, ur vår kärlek skall gå opp
Ditt ljus, din glans, din fröjd, ditt hopp,
  Och högre klinga skall en gång
  Vår fosterländska sång.

EAST INDIA.
The Gazelle.
SONG.

EGYPT.
Salaam Effindina; or, Khedival March.
NATIONAL AIR.

ECUADOR.

Salve, oh Patria.

NATIONAL SONG.

Translation by J. H. THOMAS
Versification by EDWARD M. TABER.

We sa - lute thee, and praise thee, our na - tion, Hail, all hail, Hail, all
Salve, oh Pa - tria, mit ve - ces! oh Pa - tria, gloria a ti gloria a

Hail all hail!
gloria a ti,

hail! To the land of our hearts ad - o - ra - tion, To the land of our hearts ad - o - ra - tion.
ti, ya en tu pe cho en tu pe cho re - bo - sa gora y par en tu pe cho re - bo - sa.

hail, all hail!
gloria a ti.

Joy and peace fill thy great heart for - ev - er, Till thy life blood no long - er shall
y tu fren - te y tu fren - te ra - dio - sa masque el sol con - tem - pla - mos lu -

run,.................... For the star in thy fore-head is bright - - er Than the light of the trop - i - cal
cir,.................... y tu frente, y tu fren - te ra - dio - - sa masque el sol con - tem - pla - mos lu

sun. Joy and sun. _
cir. y tu cir.

TRIO. SOLO.

Filled with righteous and fierce in - dig - na - tion, At the
In - dig - na - dos tus hi - jos del yu - go que kim

p

yoke of a deep deg - ra - da - tion, Laid by in - so - lent Spain on our na - tion, Thy brave sons raised their voice to thy
pu - so la i - berica an - da - cia, de la in - jus - ta y horrend a des - gra - cia que pe - sa - ba fatal so - bre

Chorus.

To arms, O, pa-tri-ots! And form ba-tal-lions strong, March on, march
Aux ar - mes, ce-toy-ens! For - mes vos ba-tail-lons: Mar-chons, mar.

on, Their blood im-pure shall our thres - holds bathe ere long! long!
chons, Qu'un sang im-pur a - breu - ve nos sil-lons! lons!

2.

And would that horde of slavish minions
  Conspire our freedom to o'erthrow?
Say for whom those gyves are intended
  ‖: Which their craft prepar'd long ago. :‖
What righteous rage now should excite us?
For Frenchmen what shame is so great?
They dare e'en to meditate
To enslave us:—that thought shall unite us!
    To arms, &c.

3.

Ye tyrants all, and traitors tremble!
  Ye whom each faction loads with blame;
Soon your schemes will be rewarded,
  ‖: You'll be paid the price of your shame. :‖
We all will be soldiers to meet you,
And if our young heroes must fall,
Our land will reproduce them all
Stronger yet, and ready to defeat you!
    To arms, &c.

4.

O sacred love of home and country,
  Do thou guide home each vengeful blade.
Liberty, liberty so cherish'd,
  ‖: In thy cause now give us thy aid. :‖
Beneath our flag may mighty Victory
O'erwhelm all their hosts at thy call;
And grant our cruel foes may fall
While beholding our triumph and thy glory!
    To arms, &c.

5.

May patriot love and friendship glowing
  Still be the aim to which we aspire.
May each spirit ever be lighted
  ‖: With the flame they both can inspire. :‖
All may be won; be but united,
Our foes we will crush 'neath our feet;
No more then Frenchmen will repeat
That dread cry which hath our land affrighted!
    To arms, &c.

2.

Que veut cette horde d'esclaves
  Contre nous en vain conjurés?
Pour qui ces ignobles entraves,
  ‖: Ces fers dès longtems préparés ? :‖
Français pour nous, ah quel outrage!
Quels transports il doit exiter!
C'est nous qu'on ose méditer
De rendre à l'antique esclavage?
    Aux armes, &c.

3.

Tremblez, tyrans! et vous, perfides,
  L'opprobre de tous les partis;
Tremblez! vos projets parricides
  ‖: Vont enfin recevoir leur prix. :‖
Tout est soldat pour vous combattre:
S'ils tombent nos jeunes héros,
La terre en produit de nouveaux
Contre vous tout prêts à se battre.
    Aux armes, &c.

4.

Amour sacré de la patrie,
  Conduits, soutiens nos bras vengeurs.
Liberté, liberté chérie,
  ‖: Combats avec tes défenseurs. :‖
Sous nos drapeaux que la victoire
Accoure à tes mâles accens;
Que tes ennemis expirans
Voyent ton triomphe et notre gloire.
    Aux armes, &c.

5.

Que l'amitié que la patrie,
  Fassent l'objet de tous nos vœux;
Ayons toujours l'âme remplie
  ‖: Des feux qu'ils inspirent tous deux. :‖
Soyons unis, tout est possible,
Nos vils ennemis tomberont,
Alors les Français cesseront
De chanter ce refrain terrible.
    Aux armes, &c.

"Claude Joseph Rouget De Lisle was born at Montaigu, Lons-le-Saunier, May 10, 1760. He entered the School of Royal Engineers at Mezières in 1782, and left it two years later with the rank of 'Aspirant-Lieutenant.' Early in 1789 he was made second lieutenant, and quartered at Joux, near Besançon. At Besançon, a few days after the taking of the Bastille (July 14th, 1789), he wrote his first patriotic song to the tune of a favorite air. In 1790 he rose to be first lieutenant, and was moved to Strasburg, where he soon became very popular in the triple capacity of poet, violin-player, and singer. He died, June 27, 1836."—*M. Gustave Chouquet.*

In an old volume, entitled "Essais en Vers et en prose, Par Joseph Rouget De Lisle," published in Paris in 1796, now in the Library of Congress at Washington, I found the following:

LE CHANT DES COMBATS,
VULGAIREMENT
L'HYMNE DES MARSEILLAIS
AUX MÂNES
DE SYLVAIN BAILLY
PREMIER MAIRE DE PARIS.

EXEGI MONUMENTUM, HORACE, ODE 24, LIV. 3.
STRASBURG, JOUR DE LA PROCLAMATION DE LA GUERRA.

(Here follow the stanzas of the *Marseillaise.*)—*J. P. S.*

"*The Marseillais* preserves notes of the song of glory and the shriek of death: glorious as the one, funereal like the other, it assures the country, whilst it makes the the citizen turn pale. This is its history:

There was a young officer in garrison at Strasburg named Rouget de Lisle. He was born at Lons-le-Saunier, in the *Jura*, that country of reverie and energy, as mountainous countries always are. This young man loved war like a soldier—the Revolution like a thinker. He charmed with his verses and music the slow, dull garrison life. Much in request from his two-fold talent as musician and poet, he visited the house of Dietrick, an Alsatian patriot, (*Maire of Strasbourg*), on intimate terms. Dietrick's wife and young daughters shared in his patriotic feelings, for the Revolution was advancing towards the frontiers, just as the affections of the body always commence at the extremities. They were very partial to the young officer, and inspired his heart, his poetry, and his music. They executed the first of his ideas hardly developed, confidantes of the earliest flights of his genius.

It was in the winter of 1792, and there was a scarcity in Strasburg. The house of Dietrick was poor, and the table humble; but there was always a welcome for Rouget de Lisle. This young officer was there from morning to night, like a son or brother of the family. One day, when there was only some coarse bread and slices of ham on the table, Dietrick, looking with calm sadness at De Lisle, said to him, "Plenty is not seen at our feasts; but what matter if enthusiasm is not wanting at our civic fêtes, and courage in our soldiers' hearts. I have still a bottle of wine left in my cellar. Bring it," he added, addressing one of his daughters, "and we will drink to liberty and our country. Strasburg is shortly to have a patriotic ceremony, and De Lisle must be inspired by these last drops to produce one of those hymns which convey to the soul of the people the enthusiasm which suggested it." The young girls applauded, fetched the wine, filled the glasses of their old father and the young officer until the wine was exhausted. It was midnight, and very cold. De Lisle was a dreamer: his heart was moved, his head was heated. The cold seized on him, and he went staggering to his lonely chamber, endeavoring, by degrees, to find inspiration in the palpitations of his citizen heart; and on his small clavicord, now composing the air before the words, and now the words before the air, combined them so intimately in his mind, that he could never tell which was first produced, the air or the words, so impossible did he find it to separate the poetry from the music, and the feeling from the impression. He sang everything—wrote nothing.

Overcome by this divine inspiration, his head fell sleeping on his instrument, and he did not awake until daylight. The song of the over night returned to his memory with difficulty, like the recollection of a dream. He wrote it down, and then ran to Dietrick. He found him in his garden. His wife and daughters had not yet risen. Dietrick aroused them, called together some friends as fond as himself of music, and capable of executing De Lisle's composition; Dietrick's eldest daughter accompanied them, Rouget sang. At the first verse all countenances turned pale, at the second tears flowed, at the last enthusiasm burst forth. The hymn of the country was found. Alas! it was also destined to be the hymn of terror. The unfortunate Dietrick went a few months afterwards to the scaffold to the sound of the notes produced at his own fireside, from the heart of his friend, and the voices of his daughters.

The new song, executed some days afterwards at Strasburg, flew from city to city, in every public orchestra. Marseillais adopted it to be sung at the opening and the close of the sittings of its clubs. The Marseillais spread it all over France, by singing it everywhere on their way. Hence the name of *Marseillais.* De Lisle's old mother, a royalist and religious, alarmed at the effect of her son's voice, wrote to him: "What is this revolutionary hymn, sung by bands of brigands who are traversing France, and with which our name is mingled?" De Lisle himself, proscribed as a royalist, heard it and shuddered, as it sounded on his ears, whilst escaping by some of the wild passes of the Alps. "What do they call that hymn?" he inquired of his guide. "The Marseillais," replied the peasant. It was thus he learnt the name of his own work. The arm turned against the hand that forged it. The Revolution, insane, no longer recognized its own voice. . . . It was the 'fire-water' of the Revolution, which instilled into the senses and the soul of the people the intoxication of battle."—*Lamartine.*

* * * "The thought which works voiceless in this black-browed mass, (*the Marseillese*), an inspired Tyrtæan Colonel, Rouget de Lisle, whom the earth still holds (1836) has translated into grim melody and rhythm; into his *Hymn* or *March of the Marseillese*: luckiest musical composition ever promulgated. The sound of which will make the blood tingle in men's veins; and whole Armies and Assemblages will sing it, with eyes weeping and burning, with hearts defiant of Death, Despot and Devil."—*Carlyle.*

"On the 18th Nivose (8th January, 1795), an order of the Directory enjoined that at all theatres and sights the air of the *Marseillais* should be played.

De Lisle, a son of royalist parents, and himself belonging the constitutional party, refused to take the oath to the constitution abolishing the crown; he was therefore stripped of his military rank, denounced, and imprisoned during the reign of terror, and only saved by the 9th Thermidor. He would assuredly have been accompanied to the guillotine by his own song. After the fall of Robespierre he re-entered the army, and made the campaign of La Vendée under General Hoche; was wounded, and at length, under the Consulate, returned to private life at Montaigu, where he remained in the depth of solitude and of poverty till the second Restoration. His brother then sold the little family property, and Rouget was driven to Paris; and there would have starved but for a small pension granted by Louis XVIII and continued by Louis Philippe, and for the care of his friends Béranger, David d'Angers, and especially M. and Mad. Volart, in whose house at Choisy-le-Roi he died."—*Ryde, Chouquet, et al.*

Partant pour la Syrie.
SONG.

Words by COUNT ALEXANDRE DE LABORDE.
Music by QUEEN HORTENSE.

1. When part-ing for the Ho-ly Land, Dunois, the young and brave, Be-
1. *Par-tant pour la Sy-ri-e Le jeune et beau Du-nois, Ve-*

fore the shrine of Ma - ry knelt, A bless - ing there to crave: "O
nait pri - er Ma - ri - e, De bé - nir ses ex - ploits. Fai -

grant im - mor - tal Queen a - bove, The prayer I breathe to thee, That
tes reine im - mor - tel - le! Lui dit - il en par - tant, Qu'ai -

I the fair - est fair may love, The brav - est knight may be."
mé de la plus bel - le, Je sois le plus vail - lant.

2.	2.

His oath of fealty on the stone
  He traced first with his sword;
Then followed to the battle-field
  His proud and noble lord.
There, true unto his ardent vow,
  Which flashed on high each glave,
"Love to the fairest fair," he cried,
  "And honor to the brave!"
	Il écrit sur la pierre,
	  Le serment de l'honneur,
	Et va suivre à la guerre
	  Le comte son Seigneur.
	Au noble vœu fidèle
	  Il crie en combattant:
	Amour à la plus belle,
	  Honneur au plus vaillant.

3.	3.

"To you, Dunois!" the good count said,
  "The victory we owe;
Since you my glory thus have caused,
  Henceforth you bliss shall know;
Receive my daughter Isabelle,
  A father's blessing share;
For truly, thou'rt the bravest knight,
  And she's the fairest fair."
	Viens fils de la victoire
	  Dunois, dit le Seigneur,
	Puisque tu fais ma gloire
	  Je ferai ton bonheur;
	De ma fille Isabelle
	  Sois l'époux à l'instant,
	Car elle est la plus belle
	  Et toi le plus vaillant.

4.	4.

Before Saint Mary's sacred shrine,
  Their faith they fondly prove;
And soon, with hands and hearts unite
  In bonds of holy love;
The happy throng assembled there
  A gorgeous welcome gave,
And cried, "Love to the fairest fair,"
  And "Honor to the brave!"
	A l'autel de Marie
	  Ils contractent tous deux
	Cette union chérie
	  Qui seule rend heureux;
	Chacun dans la chapelle
	  Disait en les voyant:
	Amour à la plus belle,
	  Honneur au plus vaillant.

"This popular romance dates from 1809, shortly before the battle of Wagram. The words were by Count Alexandre de Laborde, a man of lively imagination in considerable repute as a *poete di circonstance*. One evening Queen Hortense showed him a picture representing a knight clad in armor, cutting an inscription on a stone with the point of his sword, and at the request of the company he elucidated it by a little romance invented on the spot. An entreaty to put it into verse followed and Queen Hortense set the lines to music. When Louis Napoleon mounted the throne of France in 1853, his mother's little melody was recalled to mind, and although of a sentimental rather than a martial turn, it became the national air, arranged, in default of fresh words, solely for military bands."—*Chouquet.*

FRANCE.

The Parisian. (La Parisienne.)

PATRIOTIC SONG:

Words by Casimir de la Vigne.

Music by Auber.

1. Ye men of France, Ye va-liant peo - ple, Now Li - ber-ty bids you be free, Un-will-ing
2. *Peu-ple Fran-çais, peu-ple de bra - ves, La Li ber-té rou-vre ses bras, On nous di-*

slaves, ty-rants would make us, But we have said "we'll sol - diers be;" Our no-ble Pa - ris in her
sait, soy-es e-scla - ves, Nous a-vons dit "say-ons sol-dats;" Soudain Pa - ris dans sa mé-

mem - 'ry, At last re-calls her cry of glo - ry; Spite of all their guns we'll march for-ward then, E'en thro'
moi - re A re-trou-vé son cri de gloi - re; En a-vant mar-chons con-tre leurs ca-nons, A tra-

2.

Close up your ranks, firm be your bearing!
  Ye sons of France, come with open hand,
And of his cartouche let each man bravely
  An off'ring make to his native land.
These days still shall live in future story,
Paris has but one proud cry of glory!
  Spite of all their guns, &c.

3.

Ammunition in vain may devour us,
  The children of our warriors bold,
Will face the bullets of our foeman
  As dauntless as their sires of old.
These days still shall live in future story;
Paris has but one proud cry of glory!
  Spite of all their guns, &c.

4.

To destroy their deep serried masses,
  Who our flag stain'd with blood will bear?
'Tis the freedom of two worlds that passes,
  'Tis Lafayette with silver hair.
These days still shall live in future story;
Paris has but one proud cry of glory!
  Spite of all their guns, &c.

5.

The tricolor once more is sparkling;
  The column proudly bears its colors three;
Where 'twill shine tho' the clouds are darkling
  As the rainbow of our liberty.
These days still shall live in future story;
Paris has but one proud cry of glory!
  Spite of all their guns, &c.

6.

Ye drums that must beat for our brothers,
  Roll loudly with deep fun'ral tone!
The people with green deathless laurels,
  With triumph their coffins shall crown.
Oh, temple of grief and of glory,
Pantheon preserve still their story!
  We will bear them now with uncover'd brow,
  Be immortal those we weep for now,
  The martyrs of our vict'ry!
  The martyrs of our vict'ry!
    We will bear them now, &c.

2.

Serrez vos rangs qu'on se soutienne.
  Marchons! chaque enfant de Paris,
De sa cartouche citoyenne
  Fait une offrande à son pays.
O jours, d'éternelle mémoire!
Paris n'a plus qu'un cri de gloire:
    En avant, marchons, &c.

3.

La mitraille en vain nous devore,
  Elle enfante des combattans.
Sous les boulets voyez éclore
  Ces vieux généraux de vingt ans.
O jours, d'éternelle mémoire!
Paris n'a plus qu'un cri de gloire:
    En avant, marchons, &c.

4.

Pour briser leurs masses profondes,
  Qui conduit nos drapeaux sanglans?
C'est la liberté des deux mondes,
  C'est Lafayette en cheveux blancs.
O jours, d'éternelle mémoire!
Paris n'a plus qu'un cri de gloire:
    En avant, marchons, &c.

5.

Les trois couleurs sont revenues,
  Et la colonne avec fierté.
Fait briller à travers les nues
  L'arc-en-ciel de la liberté.
O jours, d'éternelle mémoire!
Paris n'a plus qu'un cri de gloire:
    En avant, marchons, &c.

6.

Tambours, du convoi de nos frères,
  Roulez le funèbre signal!
Et nous de lauriers populaires,
  Chargeons leur cercueil triomphal.
O Temple de deuil et de gloire,
Panthéon reçois leur mémoire!
  Portons les, marchons découvrons, nos fronts,
  Soyez immortels, vous tous que nous pleurons,
  Martyrs de la victoire!
  Martyrs de la victoire!
    Portons les, marchons, &c.

The Departure of the Patriots. (Le Chant du Départ.)

PATRIOTIC SONG.

3.

'Tis the sword of your sires should arm the hands of heroes,
  Let thoughts of us animate each breast;
In the hearts of vile slaves and proud tyrants consecrate then
  The steel your aged fathers have blest.
And when ye shall return you will bring us
  Your virtues and wounds to our hearth,
And peacefully our eyes ye will close then,
  When the foe is laid low in the earth.
    Chorus.—Our dear country bids us, &c.

4.

Go, ye bride-grooms so brave, and deem your war but pleasure;
  As model knights lead your valiant bands;
Fairest flow'rs we will seek far more rich than kingly treasure,
  Victorious wreaths twin'd by our hands.
And if the silent Temple of Mem'ry,
  Your ashes victorious must receive,
Our songs shall sing your valiant story,
  And our babes shall your vengeance achieve.
    Chorus.—Our dear country bids us, &c.

3.

Que le fer paternel arme la main des braves;
  Songez à nous aux champs de Mars:
Consacrez dans le sang des tyrans des esclaves
  Le fer béni par vos vieillards.
Et rapportant sous la chaumière,
  Des blessures et des vertus,
Venez fermer notre paupière
  Quand l'ennemi ne sera plus.
    Chorus.—*La Patrie amis nous, &c.*

4.

Partez, vaillans époux, les combats sont vos fêtes;
  Partez, modèles des guerriers,
Nous cueillerons des fleurs pour enceindre vos têtes;
  Nos mains tresseront vos lauriers.
Et si le temple de mémoire
  S'ouvrait à vos mânes vainquers,
Nos voix chanteront votre gloire,
  Et nos flancs portent vos vengeurs.
    Chorus.—*La Patrie amis nous, &c.*

FRANCE.

To die for Home and Country! (Mourir pour la Patrie!)
PATRIOTIC SONG.

Words by ANDRÉ CHÉNIER.

Music by ALPHONSE VARNEY.

"This song is the celebrated *Chant des Girondins*, . . . which played so important a part in the revolution of 1848."—*J. A. F. Maitland.*

NATIONAL SONG

OF

GERMAN EMPIRE—"Heil dir im Siegerkranz.
GREAT BRITAIN AND IRELAND—"God save the Queen."
BAVARIA—"Heil, unserm König, Heil!"
SWITZERLAND—"Rufst du, mein Vaterland."
BRUNSWICK, HANOVER, NORWAY, PRUSSIA, SAXONY,
WEIMAR AND WURTEMBERG.

PATRIOTIC SONG

OF

UNITED STATES OF AMERICA—"My country 'tis of thee."

GERMAN EMPIRE.

Heil dir im Siegerkranz.

Words by HEINRICH HARRIES.

Music by HENRY CAREY.

4
Handlung und Wissenschaft.
Hiebe mit Muth und Kraft,
Ihr Haupt empor!
Krieger und Heldenthat
Fende irh Lorbeerblatt,
Treu auf gehoben dort
An deinem Thron!

5.
Sei, Friedrich Wilhelm, hier,
Lang deines Volkes Zier,
Der Menschheit Stolz!
Fühl in Thrones Glanz
Die hohe Wonne ganz:
Liebling des Volks zu sein!
Heil, König, dir!

"'Heil dir im Siegerkranz,' the national song of the German Empire, was written by Heinrich Harries, a Holstein clergyman, for the birthday of Christian VII of Denmark, and published in the Flensburg Wochenblatt of Jan. 27, 1790, to the melody of the English 'God save great George, the King.' It was originally in eight stanzas, but was reduced to five and otherwise slightly modified for Prussian use by B. G. Schumacher, and in this form appeared as a 'Berliner Volkslied,' in the Spenersche Zeitung of Dec. 17, 1798."—Tappert.

BAVARIA.

"Heil, unserm Konig, Heil!"

1.
Heil, unserm König, Heil!
Dem Landesvater Heil!
 Dem König Heil!
Von Sorgen ungetrübt,
Von seinem Volk geliebt,
Herrsch' er noch lang' beglückt,
 Dem König Heil!

2.
Sei du, Gott, seine Wehr,
Dass seiner Feinde Heer
 Ibn nicht besieg';
Vernicht', was inre List
Schlau gegen den beschliesst,
Der unsre Hoffnung ist,
 Erhalt' uns ihn!

3.
O Herr, dich bitten wir,
Gesegnet stets von dir,
 Erhalt' uns ihn.
Der Bürger, dernihn ehrt,
Die Freiheit sei ihm wehrt,
So singt ein jeder froh:
 Dem König Heil!

4.
Fern sei, o Gott, sein Ziel,
Dass noch des Guten viel
 Durch ihn gescheh'.
So herrsch' er froh und frei,
Ihr Brüder, bleibt ihm treu,
Und singt vereint ihm Heil,
 Dem König Heil!

UNITED STATES OF AMERICA.

My country, 'tis of thee.

Words by Dr. S. F. Smith.

1.
My country! 'tis of thee,
Sweet land of liberty,
 Of thee I sing:
Land, where my fathers died,
Land of the pilgrim's pride,
From every mountain side
 Let freedom ring!

2.
My native country, thee,
Land of the noble free,
 Thy name I love,
I love thy rocks and rills,
Thy woods and templed hills;
My heart with rapture thrills
 Like that above.

3.
Let music swell the breeze,
And ring from all the trees
 Sweet freedom's song:
Let mortal tongues awake,
Let all that breathe partake,
Let rocks their silence break,
 The sound prolong.

4.
Our fathers' God! to thee,
Author of liberty,
 To Thee we sing:
Long may our land be bright
With freedom's holy light;
Protect us with Thy might,
 Great God, our King.

'In a letter to me, dated Newton Centre, Mass., June 11, 1861, the accomplished and estimable author says: 'The Song was written at Andover during my student life there. I think in the winter of 1831-2. It was first used publicly at a Sunday School celebration of July 4th, in Park street church, Boston. I had in my possession a quantity of German song books from which I was selecting such music as pleased me, and finding *God Save the King*, I proceeded to give it the ring of American republican patriotism.'—*Rev. Elias Nason, M. A.*

DAKOTA INDIANS.

Shice Shice Shante.
EVENING SONG.

GERMAN EMPIRE

The Watch o'er the Rhine. (Die Wacht am Rhein.)

PATRIOTIC SONG.

Words by MAX SCHNECKENBERGER. (1840.)　　　　　　　Music by C. WILHELM. (1854.)

1. With thun-der shout the air is rent, Like roar of waves and sword-clash blent "Now of the German Rhine so free, Who
1. Es braust ein Ruf wie Don-ner-hall, wie Schwertge-klirr und Wogenprall: zum Rhein, zum Rhein, zum deutschen Rhein, wer
2. The peo-ple hear that might-y cry, Like lightning flash-es ev-'ry eye, That land-mark ev-'ry heart will keep, And
2. Durch Hun-dert-tau-send zuckt es schnell, und Al-ler Au-gen bli-tzen hell, der Deut-sche bie-der, fromm und stark, be-

will the riv-er's guardian be?" Thou Fa-therland may'st tran-quil be, Thy faith-ful sons will watch o'er thee;
will des Stro-mes Hü-ter sein! Lieb Va-terland magst ru-hig sein, lieb Va-ter-land magst ru-hig sein;
watch un-sleep-ing o'er the deep.
schützt die heil'-ge Lan-des-mark.

Stead-fast and true each son, each son of thine Stands sen-try o'er our Rhine, our no-ble Rhine!
fest steht und treu die Wacht, die Wacht am Rhein! fest steht und treu die Wacht, die Wacht am Rhein!

3.
Thy tide reflects the heav'ns above,
And heroes gaze on thee with love,
And proudly breathe a vow to thee,
Thou, Rhine, shalt ever German be.
　　　　Thou, Fatherland, &c.

4.
So long as blood flows in each vein,
Or hands to draw the sword remain,
And while an arm is in the land,
No foe shall walk upon thy strand.
　　　　Thou Fatherland, &c.

5.
The waves re-echo back the cry,
The standard in the breeze doth fly,
The Rhine, the German Rhine, so free,
Yes, we will all thy guardians be.
　　　　Thou Fatherland, &c.

3.
Er blickt hinauf in Himmelsau'n,
Da Helden Väter niederschau'n,
Und schwört mit stolzer Kampfeslust,
"Du Rhein bleibst deutsch wie meine Brust."
　　　　Lieb Vaterland, &c.

4.
So lang ein Tropfen Blut noch glüht,
Noch eine Faust den Degen zieht,
Und noch ein Arm die Büchse spannt,
Betritt kein Feind hier deinen Strand!
　　　　Lieb Vaterland, &c.

5.
Der Schwur erschallt, die Woge rinnt,
Die Fahnen flattern hoch im Wind,
Am Rhein, am Rhein, am deutschen Rhein,
Wir alle wollen Hüter sein!
　　　　Lieb Vaterland, &c.

Carl Wilhelm, born at Schmalkalden, Sep. 5, 1815, and died there Aug. 26, 1873. He directed the Liedertafel at Crefeld from 1840-65. He composed the Wacht am Rhein in 1854, but it was little known until the late war between France and Germany when it suddenly became the "battle cry" of the latter. Wilhelm received an annual pension $750 for it in 1871.—Groves, et al.

GERMAN EMPIRE.

What is the German Fatherland? (Was ist des Deutschen Vaterland?)

PATRIOTIC SONG.

Words by E. M. ARNDT. (1813.)

Music by GUSTAV REICHARDT. (1825.)
(Composed for *Chorus* of Male voices.)

where the sands o'er plains are blown, Or where the Dan - ube rush - es on? O no! no!
wo der Sand der Dü - nen weht? ist's wo die Do - nau brau - send geht? Doch nein! nein!
Swit - zer - land or Ty - rol fair, The land and peo - ple please me there! O no! no!
Land der Schwei - zer, ist's Ti - rol? das Land und Volk ge - fiel mir wohl! Doch nein! nein!

no! Our Fa - ther - land must great - er be, Our Fa - ther - land must great - er be.
nein! sein Va - ter - land muss grös - ser sein, sein Va - ter - land muss grös - ser sein.

5. What is the Ger - man Fa - ther - land? Say where doth lie that fa - vor'd land? Where e'er our
5. Was ist des Deut - schen Va - ter - land? so nen - ne end - lich mir das Land! "So weit die

Ger - man ac - cents ring, And hymns to God on high they sing, 'Tis there, 'tis
deut - sche Zun - ge klingt, und Gott im Him - mel Lie - der singt," Das soll es

GERMAN EMPIRE.

Battle-cry of Freedom. (Deutscher Freiheit Schlachtruf.)

PATRIOTIC SONG.

Words by F. M. ARNDT. (1812.)　　　　　　　　　　Music by A. METHFESSEL. (1818.)

1. Our God to us gave i-ron here, That man should ne'er know slav'ry, He gave him sa-bre, sword, and spear, And
1. Der Gott, der Ei-sen wach-sen liess', der woll-te kei-ne Knechte; Drum gab er Sä-bel, Schwert und Spiess dem
2. Then let us keep our free-dom pure, And faith-ful-ly main-tain it; And nev-er for a ty-rant's gold With
2. So wol-len wir, was Gott ge-wollt, mit rech-ten Treu-en hal-ten, Und nim-mer um Ty-ran-nen-sold die

spir-it strong in brav-'ry. He gave him speech to plead his cause, In fear-less words re-veal-ing,
Mann in sei-ne Rech-te; Drum gab er ihm den küh-nen Muth, Den Zorn der frei-en Re-de,
broth-er's blood e'er stain it. Who wrong-ly fights doth best de-serve A grave un-known and go-ry:
Men-schen-schä-del spal-ten; Doch wer für Tand und Schan-de ficht, Den hau-en wir in Scher-ben,

That he should still main-tain the laws In death his faith still seal-ing.
Dass er be-stän-de bis auf's Blut, Bis in den Tod die Feh-de.
While Ger-man hands rule Ger-man lands, Let jus-tice be our glo-ry.
Der soll im deutsch-en Lan-de nicht Mit deutsch-en Män-nern er-ben.

3.
O, holy German Fatherland,
　O, love and truth unstainéd,
Our vow we here renew, fair land,
　It still shall be maintainéd.
Out-lawed may ev'ry coward fall,
　A prey to crow and raven,
But we will forth to Hermann's* field,
　And prove each heart no craven.

4.
Flash forth each bright triumphant blade,
　In heaven's pure daylight flaming;
Behold our serried ranks arrayed,
　Each coward spirit shaming.
Upraise your hands to heav'n on high,
　Let heart and voice be blended,
And man for man let each one cry,
　"Our slavery is ended!"

3.
*O Deutschland, heil'ges Vaterland,
　O deutsche Lieb' und Treue!
Du hohes Land, du schönes Land!
　Wir schwören dir auf's Neue:
Dem Buben und dem Knecht die Acht!
　Der nähre Kräh'n und Raben!
So zieh'n wir aus zur Hermannsschlacht
　Und wollen Rache haben.*

4.
*Lasst brausen, was nur brausen kann,
　In hellen, lichten Flammen!
Ihr Deutsche, alle Mann für Mann
　Zum heil'gen Krieg zusammen;
Und hebt die Herzen himmelan,
　Und himmelan die Hände,
Und ruft Alle Mann für Mann:
　"Die Knechtschaft hat ein Ende!"*

* Hermann, or Arminius, the German hero, born B. C. 18, died A. D. 20, who destroyed the Roman power in Germany.—*Trans.*

5.

Ring ont afar whate'er can ring,
  Ye clarions, trumpets blaring,
We come as brethren, man to man,
  The brunt of battle bearing,
The cowards with our swords we'll slay,
  Sweet day of wrath and glory,
Long wished for by each German heart,
  To live in future story.

6.

Bid ev'ry banner proudly wave,
  Our standards widely flying;
And man for man, if we must fall,
  In heroes' graves we're lying.
Our flag triumphant onward bear,
  Ye dauntless ranks, before ye;
We come to win our freedom here,
  Or die the death of glory.

5.

Lasst klingen, was nur klingen kann,
  Trompeten, Trommeln, Flöten!
Wir wollen heute Mann für Mann
  Mit Blut das Eisen röthen,
Mit Henker und mit Knechteblut—
  O süsser Tag der Rache!
Das klinget allen Deutschen gut,
  Das ist die grosse Sache.

6.

Lasst wehen, was nur wehen kann,
  Standarten wehn und Fahnen;
Wir wollen heut' uns Mann für Mann
  Zum Heldentode mahnen.
Auf! fliege, hohes Siegspanier,
  Voran dem kühnen Reihen!
Wir siegen oder sterben hier
  Den süssen Tod der Freien.

GREECE.

NATIONAL AIR.

GREECE.

Sons of Greece, Come, Arise!

PATRIOTIC SONG.

3.
Hark! oh, hark! Hellas maid groans beneath the yoke appalling!
Hear ye not? help! oh, help! on her sons is Hellas calling.
    To burst her bonds asunder;
    To break the yoke she's under!
    To raise towards the sky
    Proud signs of victory!—
The sword! the sword! the sword! the sword! the sword! the sword!
    To raise towards the sky
    Proud sign of victory!

4.
Oh, ye Greeks, be but brave, the barbarians despising,
They are mean, they are bad, though in endless numbers rising.
    From slavery we'll sever!
    Ah! liberty for ever!
    Now forward through the flood,
    Through foemen's crimson blood!—
The sword! the sword! the sword! the sword! the sword! the sword!
    Now forward through the flood,
    Through foemen's crimson blood!

GREAT BRITAIN AND IRELAND.

God Save the Queen.

NATIONAL SONG.

Words and Music by HENRY CAREY.

1. God save our gra-cious Queen, Long live our no-ble Queen, God save the Queen. Send her vic-to-ri-ous, Hap-py and glo-ri-ous, Long to reign o-ver us, God save the Queen.

2. O Lord, our God a-rise, Scat-ter her en-e-mies, And make them fall. Con-found their pol-i-tics, Frus-trate their knav-ish tricks, On thee our hopes we fix, O save us all.

3. Thy choic-est gifts in store, On her be pleased to pour, Long may she reign. May she de-fend our laws, And ev-er give us cause, To sing with heart and voice, God save the Queen.

"Its (God Save the Queen) first public performance is stated to have been at a dinner in 1740, to celebrate the taking of Portobello by Admiral Vernon (Nov. 20, 1739), when it is said to have been sung by Henry Carey as his own composition, both words and music.

The nearest known copy to that date is that in the "Harmonia Anglicana" of 1742 or 43, as follows. It is marked for two voices, but we give the melody only.

This is the nearest we can arrive at to the original form of the air and words, and both will be found somewhat different from those with which we are familiar. The fact that Henry Carey was the author of both is testified to by J. Christopher Smith, Handel's amanuensis, and by Dr. Harington.

In 1745 it became publicly known by being sung at the theatres as a loyal song or anthem, during the Scottish Rebellion. The Pretender was proclaimed at Edinburgh, Sep. 16, and the first appearance of "God Save the King," was at Drury Lane, Sep. 28. For a month or so it was much sung at both Covent Garden and Drury Lane; Burney harmonised it for the former, and Arne for the latter. Both words and music were printed, the latter in their present form, in the Gentleman's Magazine, Oct. 1745.

How far "God Save the King" was compiled from older airs will probably never be known. Several exist with a certain resemblance to the modern tune.—

1. An "Ayre," without further title, at p. 98 of a MS. book attributed to "Dr. Jan Bull," and dated 1619. The MS., formerly in possession of Pepusch and of Kitchener, is now in the hands of Mrs. Clark, who refuses to allow it to be seen, but the following is copied from a transcript of Sir G. Smart's;—

This is in two strains of 6 and 8 bars, and, besides its general likeness, it has both the rythm and the melody of the modern air in the first four bars of the second strain; but the minor mode makes an essential difference in the effect.

A piece, entitled "God Save the King," occurs in the same MS., p. 66, but this is founded on the phrase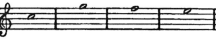

and has no resemblance whatever to the national melody.

2. A Scotch carol, "Remember, O thou man,' in Ravenscroft's "Melismata," 1611.—

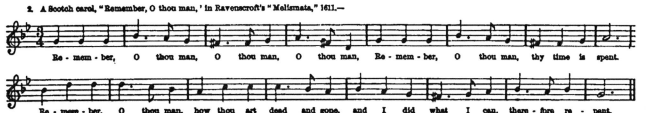

This is the air on the ground of which "God Save the King" is sometimes claimed for Scotland. It is in two strains of 8 bars each, and has the rhythm and melody of the modern tune in the first and third bars of the second strain. But it is in minor.

3. A ballad, "Franklin is Fled Away" (first printed in 1699.)—

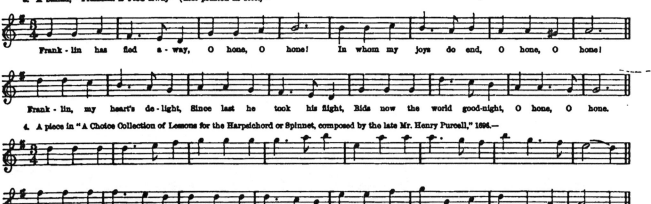

4. A piece in "A Choice Collection of Lessons for the Harpsichord or Spinnet, composed by the late Mr. Henry Purcell," 1696.—

Here the similarity is confined to the recurring rhythm in the first and third bars of each section.

Thus the rhythm and phrases of "God Save the King," and even the unequal length of the two strains (its most essential peculiarity), had all existed before. So also did some of the phrases of the words. "God Save the King" is found in the English Bible, (Coverdale, 1535), and as the phrase is in no sense a rendering of the Hebrew words, which literally are "Let the king live," it seems to follow that the phrase must have been employed in the translation as one familiar to English readers. Mr. Froude has also quoted a watchword of the navy as early as 1545—"God save the king," with the countersign, "Long to reign over us," (Hist. chap. 22.) "God save King James," is the refrain of a ballad of 1606; and "God save Charles the king, Our royal Roy, Grant him long to reign, In peace and joy," is the opening of another ballad dating probably from 1545."—*Dict. of Music and Musicians, by George Grove.*

GREAT BRITAIN AND IRELAND.

Rule Britannia!

PATRIOTIC SONG.

Words by THOMSON.

Music by DR. THOMAS AUGUSTINE ARNE.
(Born 1710, died 1778.)

1. When Bri - tain first,............... at Heav'n's com - mand, A -
2. The na - tions not............... so blest as thee, Must

rose.................. from out the a - - zure main, A - rose, a - rose, a - rose from out the
in............................ their turn to ty - - rants fall, Must in their turn.................. to

a - zure main, This was the char - ter, the char - ter of the land, And
ty - rants fall; While thou shalt flour - ish, shall flour - ish great and free, The

"The music of this noble ode in honor of Great Britain,—which, according to Southey, will be the political hymn of this country (England), as long as she maintains her political power,—was composed by Arne for his masque of "Alfred" (the words by Thomson and Mallet), and first performed at Cliefden House, Maidenhead, Aug. 1, 1740. Cliefden was then the residence of Frederick, Prince of Wales, and the occasion was to commemorate the accession of George I, and the birthday of Princess Augusta."—*William Chappell, F. S. A.*

guar - dian an - - - - gels sung this strain: " Rule, Bri - tan - nia! Bri -
dread and ev - - - - ry of them all. " Rule, Bri - tan - nia! Bri -

tan - nia, rule the waves; Bri - tons nev - - - er will be slaves."

Chorus to be sung after each verse.
SOPRANO.

ALTO.
Rule, Bri - tan - nia! Bri - tan - nia, rule the waves; Bri - tons nev - - er will be slaves.
TENOR.

BASS.
Rule, Bri - tan - nia! Bri - tan - nia, rule the waves; Bri - tons nev - - er will be slaves.

3.
Still more majestic shalt thou rise,
  More dreadful from each foreign stroke;
As the loud blast, that tears the skies,
  Serves but to root thy native oak.
    Rule, Britannia! &c.

4.
Thee haughty tyrants ne'er shall tame;
  All their attempts to bend the down,
Will but arouse thy gen'rous flame,
  To work *their* woe, and *thy* renown.
    Rule, Britannia! &c.

5.
To thee belongs the rural reign,
  Thy cities shall with commerce shine.
All thine, shall be the subject main,
  And ev'ry shore it circles, *thine.*
    Rule, Britannia! &c.

6.
The muses, still with freedom found,
  Shall to thy happy coast repair;
Blest Isle! with matchless beauty crown'd,
  And manly hearts to guard the fair.
    Rule, Britannia! &c.

GAUTEMALA.

Gautemala, around thy free banner. (Guatemala, en tu limpia bandera.)

NATIONAL SONG.

Letra de Dn. Ramon P. Molina.

Música del Psor. Dn. Rafael Alvarez.

1. Gau-te-ma-la, around thy free ban-ner Li-ber-
2. *Gau-te-ma-la, en tu lim-pia ban-de-ra Li-ber-*

ty has e-rect-ed its shrine; Li-ber-ty is the crown of thy glo-ry, For A-mer-i-ca's free sun is thine.
tad te formó un ar-re-bol; Li-ber-tad es tu glo-ria he-chi-ce-ra, Y de A-mé-ri-ca li-bre es el Sol!

Beau-teous land, to thy glo-ry we proud-ly sing, With a pas-sion both warm and sub-lime, For sweet
Civ-il li-ber-ty is thine for-ev-er-more, Reason's law is the law and the right, On-ward,
Bel-la Pa-tria, tu glo-ri-a can-ta-mos, Con ar-dien-te su-bli-me ansie-dad, Hoy que
De-mo-cra-cia, ci-vis-mo, es tu le-ma, La igual-dad es tu ley, tu ra-són No más

li-ber-ty's star shines up-on thy brow, With a splen-dor undimmed by age or time.
com-rades, to work for our coun-try's good, And hur-rah for the Un-ion in its might.
lu-ce en tu fren-te la auro-ra, De la her-mo-sa, fe-lis li-ber-tad!
som-bras, no más re-tro-ce-sos; Vi-va Pa-tria, el dere-cho y la Unión!

DUET.

2.

Under aegis of progress and plentitude,
  Peace and prosperity will be thine;
Gautemala, O link in thy dear embrace
  All thy sons in a band of love divine.
Thy Olympian brow now is grandly crowned
  With the circlet of true liberty,
And the love of thy daughters divine has made
  Gautemala an Eden of the Free.

CHORUS.

Gautemala, around thy free banner, &c.

DUET.

3.

Spartan-like in thy noble and happy state,
  Fame awaits thee, for progress is king!
Look ahead to glory that must be thine,
  In the future 'twill more greatness bring.
Sons of freemen, now greet thee, O motherland,
  With ovations both true and sincere;
May the prayers of our hearts always be with thee,
  O, our country to us forever dear!

CHORUS.

Guatemala, around thy free banner, &c.

DUO.

2.

¡Bajo la tjida libre y fecunda,
De progreso, de pas, de igualdad,
Guatemala que se unan tus hijos,
En abrazos de eterna amistad!
  La más pura y felis democracia,
Que corone tu olímpica sien;
Y, al amor de tus hijas divinas,
Sî de América libre el Edén!

CORO.

¡Guatemala, en tu limpia bandera, &c.

DUO.

3.

¡Con tu aliento gentil de Espartana,
Llegarás en el mundo á lucir,
Porque marchas buscando el progreso,
Y en tu idea se ve el porvenir!
  ¡De los libres recibe el saludo,
Su entusiasta sincera ovación;
Y recibe las preces del alma,
Los afectos del fiel corazón!

CORO.

¡Guatemala, en tu limpia bandera, &c.

HINDOOSTAN.
TYPICAL AIR.

HAWAII.

Our Native Land. (Hawaii ponoi.)

NATIONAL AIR.

Words by KING KALAKAUA.
Translation by HENRY L. SHELDON.

Composed by H. BERGER.
Musical Director Hawaiian Government Band.

1. Ha - wa - ii! sea - girt land! Strong for thy mon - arch stand, Sons of the an - cient band, Stand for your King!
1. Ha - wa - ii po - no - i Na - na - i kou Mo - i Ka la ni A - lii, Ke A - li - i.

2. Ha - wa - ii's true - born sons Cher - ish the high - born ones, From old their lin - e - age runs, Guard the young chiefs.
2. Ha - wa - ii po - no - i Na - na - i na' li - i Na - pu a muli kou Na po ki - i.

3. Ha - wa - ii! young and brave, Thine 'tis thy - self to save! Hopeful thy ban - ners wave— Up - ward and on.
3. Ha - wa - ii po - no - i E ka la - hui e O kau ha - na nui E u - i e.

O Thou who reign'st a - bove, Fa - ther of might and love, Grant that Thy peaceful dove Brood o'er our land. land.
Ma ku a la ni e Ka me ha - me - ha e Na ka ua e pa - le Me ka i - he. he.

HONDURAS.

Dios Salve a Honduras.

NATIONAL AIR.

By Lauroano Campos.

HOLLAND.

Wien Nierlansch.

NATIONAL SONG.

3.
Preserve, oh God, the dear old ground
  Thou to our fathers gave;
The land where we a cradle found,
  And where we'll find a grave!
We call, oh Lord, to Thee on high,
  As near death's door we stand.
Oh! safety, blessing, is our cry,
  ‖: For Prince and Fatherland. :‖

4.
Loud ring thro' all rejoicings here,
  Our pray'r, oh Lord, to Thee!
Preserve our Prince, his House, so dear
  To Holland, great and free!
From youth thro' life, be this our song,
  Till near to death we stand:
Oh God, preserve our sov'reign long,
  ‖: Our Prince and Fatherland. :‖

HOLLAND.

"Flanders."

PATRIOTIC SONG.

Richard Hol.

3.
Thy looms through many ages,
Were o'er the world renowed,
And praised in history's pages,
Thy rich and fertile ground;
Dost high above each neighbour,
In art and talent stand;
Oh! land of fruitful labour,
‖: My Flemish land! :‖

4.
No tumults here are raging,
No foes have we to fear;
The wars our sire were waging,
Have gained us freedom here!
Our fathers then who perished,
In dear remembrance stand,
Oh! honored, loved, and cherished,
‖: My Flemish land! :‖

5.
Submissive is our nation,
Although from cringing free,
'Tis filled with veneration,
For law and liberty,—
Her children guard with bravery
Their freedom's precious band,
Oh! free from every slavery,
‖: My Flemish land! :‖

6.
Oh! Father we implore Thee,
Thy gifts on us bestow,
Let, as we kneel before Thee,
Thy blessings on us flow!
Oh! Thou who failed us never,
Spread still o'er us Thy hand,
And guard our dear land ever,
‖: My Flemish land! :‖

This song was composed for an open competition of Dutch national songs, and obtained the first prize at Ghent, 1869.

HOLLAND.

William of Nassau.

PATRIOTIC SONG.

(A. D. 1568.)

1. Of Nas - sau, and O - ra - nia, A true Dutch prince am I; The crown of fair His - pa - nia I ev - er
2. My faith in God nought's moving, I know that I shall reign, If He's of me ap - prov - ing, O'er my dear
3. How ma - ny knights have giv - en For ye their no - ble blood, And I have ev - er striv - en To reign as

hon - our'd high; My Fa - ther - land I guard - ed With mild and faith - ful hand; Yet
land a - gain. Oh, Neth - er - lands, to save ye, My life, my all, I'd yield, As
Chris - tain good. From faith I ne'er will sev - er, Thou, Lord, shalt be my shield; A -

now.......... I am dis - card - ed, Am robb'd of crown and land!
brave.......... A - dol - phus gave ye His life on Fries - land's field!
gainst......... op - pres - sion ev - er My faith - ful sword I'll wield!

4.
Oh, Netherlands, on turning
To ye my proud heart bleeds;
My royal blood is burning
At Spaniard's coward deeds.
The lands in my possession
Are wasting, I must flee!
Oh Lord, from Spain's oppression
Help me my people free!

5.
To God, the Lord of power,
Trust Christian-like the fight,
And He in danger's hour
Will sure defend the right.
I ne'er, I vow to Heaven,
Despised the king of Spain;
I but what God has given
In justice would retain!

"William of Nassau," and "The Tithe," are good specimens of a numerous class of Dutch songs which owe their origin to the time when the Duke of Alva was sent to the Netherlands, armed by Philip II., with the most absolute power over the unhappy country, to mercilessly extinguish the rising flame of religious reformation and political independence. In the admirable work of J. F. Williams: "Oude Vlaemsche Liederen, ten deele de Melodiën," Ghent, a number of these lyrics are preserved. The songs are nearly all of great length, "William of Nassau" consists of 15 verses, though greatly condensed, the version given here preserves the sense of the whole.

HOLLAND.

The Tithe.

OLD DUTCH PATRIOTIC SONG.

(A. D. 1570.)

3.
He draws from each his dearest good,
Keeps it himself, and even would
‖: Quell freedom in our nation! :‖
He robs us men, or sheds our blood,
Or takes our reputation!

4.
Yet they who faith in him conserve,
Must money, blood, the God they serve,
‖: Soon unto him surrender; :‖
Who give him much dare nought reserve,
The tithe they too must tender!

5.
Take often one from ten, you'll see,
At last not much will over be.
‖: This wolf not only taketh, :‖
The shepherd, wool, and milk, but he
The sheep's poor back e'en breaketh!

6.
His savage hunger quits him ne'er,
Gold, gold and blood his whole thoughts share;
‖: When he between them chooseth, :‖
Before he'll yield, the money e'er
E'en royal blood he loseth!

7.
Does he deserve the tithe to take?
On all your goods a profit make,
‖: In word and deed deceiving? :‖
If ye give in ye'll never break
The bonds ye now are weaving!

8.
Ye bear all meekly, Netherlands!
What death in life before ye stands!
‖: Serve tyrants of Hispania? :‖
Or place your cause within the hands
Of our own prince Orania!

See foot-note to previous song.

HUNGARY
NATIONAL SONG.

1. Swear, Hun-ga-rian, by thy country, Thou'lt through ev-'ry fate stand fast, Let the land in birth thy cra-dle,
2. Ho-ly is the ground, oh, children, Where once flow'd your fa-ther's blood; Land where saintly homes and no-ble
3. Free-dom, ha! thy blood-y ban-ner, Led to bat-tles fierce of yore, In the field our no-blest he-roes

Form thy grave for thee at last. Thou wilt ne'er find place of rest-
Through a thou-sand years have stood. In our coun-try fought with glo-
Fell for thee, to rise no more. Though struck down by need and trou-

ing, If to oth-er lands dost hie, Though thy lot be
ry, Ar-pad's* ho-ly he-ro band, Hun yad's† might-y
ble, Though now dimm'd is free-dom's light, Lives our na-tion

Hungarian National Music possesses a most decided character of its own. Peculiarity of melodic, as well as rhythmic construction, gives it a charm of most distinctive originality. The songs are mostly of a plaintive or melancholy character, sometimes of a fiery merriment; rarely do they express a placid sentiment.

The Hungarian Dance Music (best played by the native Gipsy bands possessing no knowledge of the science of music), frequently turns from the strains of exquisitely expressed melancholy, abruptly to the very extreme of wild merriment, and no description can convey an idea of the effect of these wild modulations, if accomplished with that delicacy of ear and refinement, for which these native bands are celebrated.

One of the Rhythmic peculiarities is the frequent syncopation of the second note :— which is due in a great measure to the Hungarian language. The ending phrase is mostly like :— or, which should be distinctly accented.

Unfortunely the pronunciation of the English language offers serious obstacles to the translator, and the charm of the wild poetry is lost in the process of fitting words to the music.—*Kappey, in Songs of Eastern Europe.*

* Arpad, or Duke Stephen, the "apostolic king," (afterwards the patron saint of Hungary), founded in 997 the first dynasty of Hungarian monarchs. The Arpadian line ruled in Hungary till the year 1301.

† John Hunyad (named Corvin) waiwode of Transylvania, courageously defended Hungary against the Ottomans during the minority of Ladislas V. Hunyad died in 1455.

joy, or sor-row, Here, oh   true Hun-ga-rian, live and die!   4. Ah! great world, thou home of na-tions, Turn to-wards us
arm once shatter'd Shame-ful   yokes, which bent the Father-.land.   5. God E - ter - nal, rock of Hung'ry, Let us not as
bent, not broken, By the   ma - ny foe's re-sist-less might.   6. Swear, Hunga - rian, t'wards thy country Faith un-wav-er-

in   our need, Thousand years of   suf-f'ring pray thee, As to life, or death we lead, Hearts of   he-roes
per-ish'd be, Let the gold-en   time be   dawn-ing Mil-lions now be-seech of thee, If it   come not,
ing   to   keep, Let her earth which now doth nour-ish Guard thee in the last   long sleep; Oth - er   lands, oh!

for   their   coun - try,   Nev - er   ought to   bleed in   vain;
the.1, if   need - ful,   Let   us   fall as   he-roes brave,
true   Hun - ga - rian,   Bid   no   rest - ing place to thee,

Ne'er should breasts of   faith - ful chil - dren,   Fruit - less   burst with   pa - triot's burn - ing   pain.
Let through seas   of   blood our king - dom   No - bly   swim at   last to - wards the   grave.
Hold thy home thy   rock and trea - sure,   What - so -   e'er thy   fate in   it may   be.

IRELAND.

The Minstrel-Boy.

PATRIOTIC SONG.

Words by Thomas Moore.

Air—"The Moreen."

1. The Min-strel-boy to the war is gone, In the ranks of death you'll find him; His fa-ther's sword he has gird-ed on, And his wild harp slung be-hind him. "Land of song!" said the war-rior-bard, "Tho' all the world be-trays thee, One sword at least, thy rights shall guard, One faith-ful harp shall praise thee!"

2. The Min-strel fell! but the foe-man's chain Could not bring his proud soul un-der; The harp he loved ne'er spoke a-gain, For he tore its cords a-sun-der; And said, "No chains shall sul-ly thee, Thou soul of love and brav-er-y! Thy songs were made for the pure and free, They shall nev-er sound in slav-er-y!"

IRELAND.

Let Erin remember the days of old.

PATRIOTIC SONG.

Words by THOMAS MOORE.

Air—"THE RED FOX."

In moderate time.

1. Let E-rin remem-ber the days of old, Ere her faith-less sons be-tray'd her; When Ma-la-chi wore the col-lar of gold,* Which he won from her proud in-vad-er; When her kings, with standard of green un-furl'd, Led the Red-Branch knights to dan-ger; Ere the em'rald gem of the west-ern world Was set in the crown of a stran-ger.

2. On Lough Neagh's bank, as the fisherman strays,† When the clear cold eve's de-clin-ing, He sees the round tow'rs of oth-er days In the wave be-neath him shin-ing; Thus shall mem-'ry oft-en, in dreams sub-lime, Catch a glimpse of the days that are o-ver; Thus sigh-ing, look thro' the waves of time For the long fad-ed glo-ries they cov-er.

* "This brought on an encounter between Malachy, the monarch of Ireland in the tenth century, and the Danes, in which Malachy defeated two of their champions, whom he encountered successively, hand to hand—taking a collar of gold from the neck of one, and carrying off the sword of the other, as trophies of his victory."—*Warner's History of Ireland. Vol. 1, Book 9.*

† "It was an old tradition, in the time of Gualdus, that Lough Neagh had been originally a fountain, by whose sudden overflowing the country was inundated, and a whole region, like the Atlantis of Plato, overwhelmed. He says that the fishermen, in clear weather, used to point out to strangers the tall ecclesiastical towers under the water."—*Mooney.*

IRELAND.

The harp that once thro' Tara's halls.

PATRIOTIC SONG.

Words by Thomas Moore.

Air—"Gramachree."

Andante.

Con espressione.

1. The harp that once thro'
2. No more to chiefs and

Ta - ra's halls, The soul of mu - sic shed; Now hangs as mute on Ta - ra's walls, As if that soul were
la - dies bright, The harp of Ta - ra swells: The chord a - lone, that breaks at night, Its tale of ru - in

fled, So sleeps the pride of for - mer days, So glo - ry's thrill is o'er, And hearts, that once beat
tells. Thus free - dom now so sel - dom wakes The on - ly throb she gives, Is when some heart in -

high for praise, Now feel that pulse no more..........
dig - nant breaks, To show that still she lives..........

Tara's Hill was beautifully situated about four miles from Navar, on the Dublin road. Many centuries ago an immense palace stood on this spot, and every year, during the first week of November, the kings and other prominent persons were accustomed to meet for the purpose of making laws, and enjoying festivals, etc., enlivened by music. This tune is one of the oldest Irish airs, known as "Gramachree," and was originally sung to "Adown on Banna's banks I strayed."—*Gardner's Music of Nature, et al.*

IRELAND.

Oh, for the swords of former times!

PATRIOTIC SONG.

Words by Thomas Moore.

Allegro con spirito.

1. Oh, for the swords of former time! Oh, for the men who bore them, When
2. Oh, for the Kings who flourish'd then! Oh, for the pomp that crown'd them, When

arm'd for Right, they stood sublime, And tyrants crouch'd before them! When free yet, ere courts began With honors to en-slave him, The
hearts and hands of free-born men, Were all the ramparts round them! When safe built on bo-soms true, The throne was but the cen-tre, Round

best honors worn by man, Were those which virtue gave him. Oh, for the swords of former time! Oh, for the men who bore them, When
which, love a cir-cle drew That treason durst not en-ter. Oh, for the Kings who flourish'd then! Oh, for the pomp that crown'd them, When

ad lib.

arm'd for Right they stood, sub-lime, And ty-rants crouch'd be-fore them!
hearts and hands of free-born men, Were all the ram-parts round them!

colla voce.

f con spirito.

ISTRIA.

Beautiful Istria. (Oll Istria.)

NATIONAL AIR.

By Giulio Georgieri.

side. On thy hil - locks so ver-dant and love-ly, Far off stran-gers now wist - ful - ly gaze, For thy
far. Quai sme - ral - di i tuoi pin-gui oli - ve - ti Sono in - vi - dia al lon - ta - no stra - nier, So - no

vine - yards so fruit - ful and home - ly, Are the ob - jects of en - vy and praise. To thy
sem - pre i tuoi dol - ci vi - gne - ti nuo - va - fon - te di vita e pia - cer. Del - le

fair coasts, O Is - tria, the mu - ses Bring thy off - spring both knowledge and fame, On their
mu - se qui il mi - te, sor - ri - so, qui il sa - pe - re ebbe cul - to ed o - nor; a' tuoi

The muses there have often smiled on thy fair coast and hon - or
Del - le mu - se sor - ri - so eb - be cul - to ed o - nor

Con espressione.

ITALY.

The Royal March and Fanfare.

NATIONAL AIR.

By G. GABETTI.

ITALY.

The Volunteer's Farewell. (L'addio del Voluntario.)

FLORENTINE PATRIOTIC SONG.

1. Fare - well, my love, I leave thee, Our fleet must now de -
2. Ad - dio mia bel - la, ad - di - o L'ar - ma - ta se ne

part,.............. Fare - well, my love, I leave thee, Our fleet must now de -
vả,.............. Ad - dio mia bel - la, ad - di - o, L'ar - ma - ta se ne

part;.............. Should I not go, be - lieve me, 'Twould show a cow - ard
vả;.............. Se non par - tis - se an - ch'i - o, Sa - reb - be u - na vil -

heart;............. Should I not go, be-lieve me, 'Twould show a cow-ard

tà;................. Se non par-tis-si an-ch'i-o, Sa-reb-be u-na vil-

Last Time.

heart................

tà......................

2.	2.
My sack and my good pistols	*Il sacco e le pistole*
And gun I take with me,	*Lo schioppo io l'ho con me;*
And at the dawn of morning	*Allo spuntar del sole*
I must depart from thee.	*Io partirò da te.*
3.	3.
Then dry thy tears, my darling,	*Asciuga o bella il ciglio,*
Grief is the coward's plea;	*Sol dei codardi è il duol,*
To die is but the duty	*Chi dell' Italia è figlio*
Of each son of Italy.	*Muora pel patrio suol.*
4.	4.
It is no civil warfare	*Non è fraterna guerra,*
I go forth to maintain;	*La guerra ch'io farò*
It is to drive the alien*	*Dall' Italiana terra*
From the soil which now they stain.	*L'estraneo* scaccerò.*
5.	5.
Then do not weep thus vainly,	*Non pianger mio tesoro,*
I may return, my love,	*Forse ritornerò,*
But if I'm slain in battle	*E se in battaglia moro*
We'll meet in heav'n above.	*In ciel ti rivedrò.*
6.	6.
And Fame will there be seated	*Alla mia tomba appresso,*
Upon my glorious tomb,	*La gloria sederà.*
And instead of mournful cypress	*E invece del cipresso*
A flower there will bloom.	*Un fior vi spunterà.*
7.	7.
This flow'r, my well beloved,	*Quel fiore, idolo amato,*
Will bear the colors three;	*I tre colori avrà,*
Embrace it, for 'twill spring from	*Bacialo e di ch'è nato,*
A soil that will be free!	*In suol di libertà!*
8.	8.
We'll rend the black and yellow,†	*Si stracci il giallo e nero,†*
Symbol of grief and dread	*Simbolo del dolor;*
And proudly shall the Italians	*E l' Italiano altero*
Raise the tricolor ‡ instead!	*Inalzi il tricolor!‡*

*The Austrians.   †The Austrian colors.   ‡The Italian colors—green, white, and red.

ITALY.

The Tricolored Banner. (La Nocca de Tre Colure.)

NEAPOLITAN PATRIOTIC SONG.

2. 'Tis for hope the green that you behold here,
   Which we sigh'd for so long,
   That it well nigh turn'd off mouldy
   Ere our liberty we won.
   If you don't believe it's true,
   I will prove it soon to you.

3. Next, the white which here you see so pure and simple,
   Tells its meaning to all;
   'Tis that all men here are equal,
   We are brothers,—and that's all.
   He who tells this tale to you,
   He has seen and knows 'tis true.

4. Last, the crimson 'neath whose splendour,
   We to vict'ry have been led,
   Signifies our joy and triumph
   Wild enough to turn each head.
   This was told to me as true,
   Even so I tell it you.

5. 'Mong triumphant wreaths and brightest flowers,
   Our cockade will brightly shine;
   And thrice blest shall be the colors,
   And our liberty divine!
   Let us shout and loudly cheer
   Now we have no cause of fear.

2. *Chillo vverde è la speranza,*
   Che nce a fotto assennecà
   E perimma inta a la pansa
   Nce ave fatto fravecà;
   Tanto stiente ne pecchè
   Sto colore, ppe vedè.

3. *Sa lo janco è assaje carnale*
   Ne che buà segnificà
   Ca nuje simmo tutt' eguale
   Simmo frate e basta ca;
   Chi l'aveise ditto a tte
   Chesti ccose de vedè.

4. *E llo rrusso che po spezza*
   Tanto bbello mmiezo llà
   E la gioja, la priezza
   Che nce fa svertecellà.
   Chesto ditto m'hanno a mme
   Io lo dico purzì a te.

5. *'Nfra, masse de lli sciure*
   Mosta Nocca stanno a fà
   Beneditte lli colure
   E la bella libertà,
   Va allaccammo mena me
   Ca paura cchiu non nè è.

IROQUOIS INDIANS.

Ige Ige.

WAR SONG.

ITALY.

Garibaldi's Hymn. (Inno di Guerra dei Cacciatori Delle Alpi.)

Words by LUIGI MERCANTINI.

Tempo di marcia.

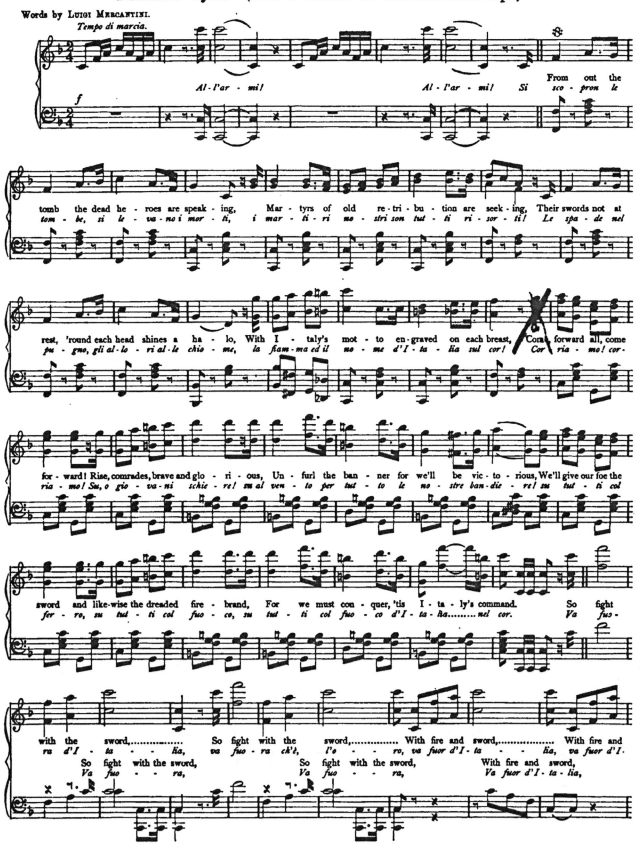

sword,................   With fire and with sword.
ta - - lia,   *va fuo - ra, o stra - nier!*
With fire and sword,
va fuor d' I - ta - lia,

IOWA INDIANS.
SQUAW DANCE.

Dja de wi dje ha ke i he g'a dja de wi dje ha ke i he g'a wa coñ ta yañ i dje ha ke dje de we dje ha ke i he g'a.

LAPLAND.
TYPICAL AIR.

JAMAICA.

Kalimba, or Pepper Pot.
NATIONAL AIR.

The following words are usually sung to the national air of Jamaica:—

Monkey, monkey play the fiddle;
Monkey, monkey play the fiddle,
Monkey, monkey play the fiddle,
Make de baboon dance.

JAPAN.

Fou sô ka.

NATIONAL AIR.

JAPAN.

Song of the Boatmen.

JAPAN.

Kimygayo.

TYPICAL AIR.

"The popular music of Japan has remained for many centuries in the hands of the lowest and most ignorant classes of society. It did not advance moral or physical culture, but was altogether immoral in tone. It is against the moral and social welfare of the community. It is against the progress of the education of society. It is against the introduction of good music into the country. But unfortunately all children are taught this kind of music, even though they are not sent to school; and it is not uncommon for the people to refuse to listen to good music, but to prefer such shameful Music as that under consideration.

"While such music keeps its influence, schools are of little use to the country, however numerous they may be; and education is of little use to society, however good it may be. Now what can be done about this popular music, is a great problem to be solved by the enlightened classes of society. Some say it must be entirely forbidden, others say it should be permitted only for the lower classes, and should be forbidden for the upper classes, and yet others say the old music should be put an end to, and new music should be introduced. All these proposals are impracticable, though in some cases they may seem reasonable. Then the question naturally follows, is there no way to deal with the popular music? Yes; there is. Such popular music as is so deeply rooted in the hearts of the people, cannot be eradicated entirely, but may be revised by degrees. The Institute has already taken a step towards this end, but it has not yet been fully carried out, in consequence of there being so many things to do after the establishment of the Institute. The Institute, however, having been now brought into good working order, and the system of school music founded on a firm basis, the time has come when the full energy of the Institute can be applied to the solution of the question.

"The process by which the popular music should be revised, is itself quite simple. Though the condition of popular music is as stated above, it is a corrupted condition, and not an original state. The original music was comparatvely pure, that is, far better than it is at present. Moreover, all kinds of the popular music are not corrupted to the same degree. Among others, *Koto* music seems to be almost free from corruption, and even in this music, the oldest is the purest. Therefore, the revision was begun in this class of music because the advantage is two-fold ;—first, the work can be done with far less labor ; secondly, with more certainty of success.

"When this work is taken in hand, the materials for the revision are selected particularly from the oldest forms by a committee. After their report, a general council is held on a certain day to determine whether the piece is fit for revision or not. The music, as well as the words, is tried by a concert of *Koto, Kokiu, Siamsin, Shakuhachi,* &c. If the music is good and the words are not, the words are revised, but if both music and words are unsuitable the piece is rejected. After the words are reformed, a trial will be made again by the same concert as before. On this trial, if the words are found unfit for the music, they will be corrected or revised, again and again, until all is right.

"In the next place, the revision of *Nagauta* has been commenced, and is conducted, in the same way as in the case of *Koto* music. However, time and space do not allow us to enter into any detail. The difficulty experienced in these revisions is not to compose better words, not to make better music, but to construct old pieces by adapting the music and words to each other as perfectly as may be; no matter how complicated the music, or how long and complex the phrases may be.

"When a piece is finished after passing the various steps above enumerated, it is harmonized, so far as the natural beauty of Japanese music can be retained, according to the principles of modern music, in order to make it on an equality with European music. Notwithstanding the many difficulties which have occurred in the way of this revision, a great many pieces have already been finished. Some of these were played at the Musical Exhibition held for reporting the result of the investigations on Music by the Institute, and on many other occasions since that time.

"There are many advantages in this revised music which may facilitate its extensive use in future. It is written on a staff of five lines, with the modern notation,—a work never attempted before,—which makes the teaching of this music very much easier than the old method, which depended entirely on rote teaching, having no help whatever from the notation."

"The text books and music readers will be published soon after they are approved by the authorities. As soon as these publications are ready, instruction will commence for the students attached to the Institute, in the Girls' Normal School, and in private schools taught by those who are actually engaged in this revision. Some special arrangements will be made for those who wish to learn particularly this kind of music, and some other means will be adopted for its farther diffusion through the country. After this is done, the old immoral music will be forbidden. Then the new works will soon displace the old ones, because this revised music conforms to the theory of science and art, as well as to the principles of morality, so that its prospects of success are already very bright."—*Extracts from the Report of S. Isawa, Director of the Institute of Music, on the result of the investigations concerning music, undertaken by order of the Departments of Education, Tokio, Japan.*

Second month of the 17th year of Meiji.

JAPAN.
Fuki.
KOTO MUSIC.

Arr. by S. Yamase.

JAVA.

Push and Row. (Surung Dayung.)

BOAT SONG.

LAPLAND.

Reindeer, galop fast.
TYPICAL. SONG.

Andante, non troppo lento.

1. Rein - deer, gal - lop fast O - ver mount and plain, Till the tent we gain, And my love at last;
2. Ah! how short the day, And the roads how long, Come, let mer - ry songs Short - en now our way;
3. Ah! yon ea - gle see! Could I with him hie, Like the cloud - lets fly, From all sor - row free!
4. Rest I seek in vain; Thousand mad de - sires, Like de - vour - ing fires, Fill my throb - bing brain!

To the for - est haste, There green moss shalt taste! To the for - est haste, There green moss shalt free!
Fly, my rein - deer, here, Wolves are howl - ing near! Fly my rein - deer, here, Wolves are howl - ing near!
Then my eyes could rove Un - to thee, oh love! Then my eyes could rove Un - to thee, oh love!
Each one cries to thee, "Give thy heart to me!" Each one cries to thee, "Give thy heart to me!"

LITHUANIA.

The Bride's Farewell.
TYPICAL SONG, OR DAINA.

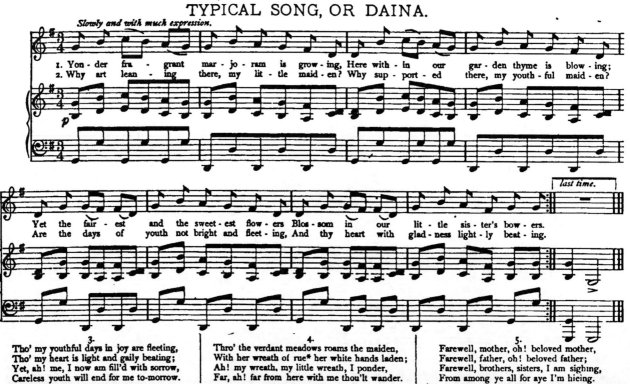

Slowly and with much expression.

1. Yon - der fra - grant mar - jo - ram is grow - ing, Here with - in our gar - den thyme is blow - ing;
2. Why art lean - ing there, my lit - tle maid - en? Why sup - port - ed there, my youth - ful maid - en?

Yet the fair - est and the sweet - est flow - ers Blos - som in our lit - tle sis - ter's bow - ers.
Are the days of youth not bright and fleet - ing, And thy heart with glad - ness light - ly beat - ing.

last time.

3.
Tho' my youthful days in joy are fleeting,
Tho' my heart is light and gaily beating;
Yet, ah! me, I now am fill'd with sorrow,
Careless youth will end for me to-morrow.

4.
Thro' the verdant meadows roams the maiden,
With her wreath of rue* her white hands laden;
Ah! my wreath, my little wreath, I ponder,
Far, ah! far from here with me thou'lt wander.

5.
Farewell, mother, oh! beloved mother,
Farewell, father, oh! beloved father;
Farewell, brothers, sisters, I am sighing,
From among ye all for aye I'm hieing.

* Rue, (Ruta graveolans,) is very frequently mentioned in the folklore of the different nations of the north and east of Europe. In the traditional songs of Lithuania, Finland, Esthonia, etc., it forms a poetic symbol of moral purity, as the myrtle does with us; hence the path of a bride is "strewn with rue," or she wears a "wreath of rue." But in Eastern Europe, in Servia, Bulgaria, etc., it is a symbol of woe, and the binding of a wreath of rue portends misfortune or death.

Daina (pl. Dainos), Lithuanian term for secular song, in contradistinction to Gésme—sacred or religious song."—*Songs of Northern Europe.*

LIBERIA.

All hail, Liberia, hail!

NATIONAL SONG.

By Olmstead Luca.

LUXEMBURG.

March of the Arabesques.

PATRIOTIC AIR.

MADEIRA ISLANDS.

TYPICAL AIRS.

MALTA.

Diáisá Maltese.

PATRIOTIC AIR.

MARHATTA.

TYPICAL AIR.

MARTINIQUE.

TYPICAL AIRS.

These airs were sent to the compiler, by Mr. Wm. A. Garesché, U. S. Consul at Martinique, who states they are Creole airs indigenous to that Island, and not procurable in print.

MARTINIQUE.

No. 3.

D.C.

FINE.

MARTINIQUE.

169

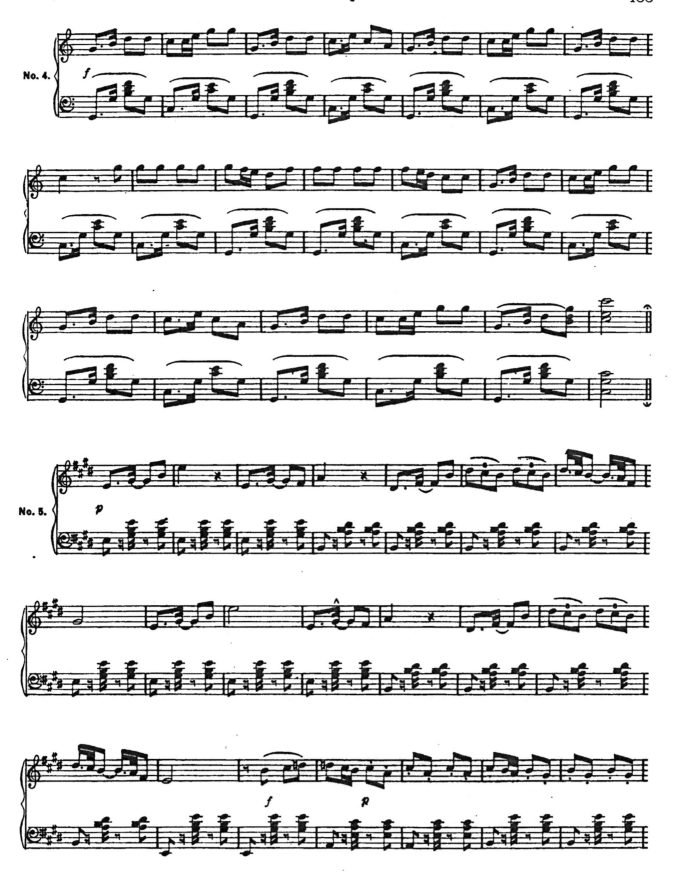

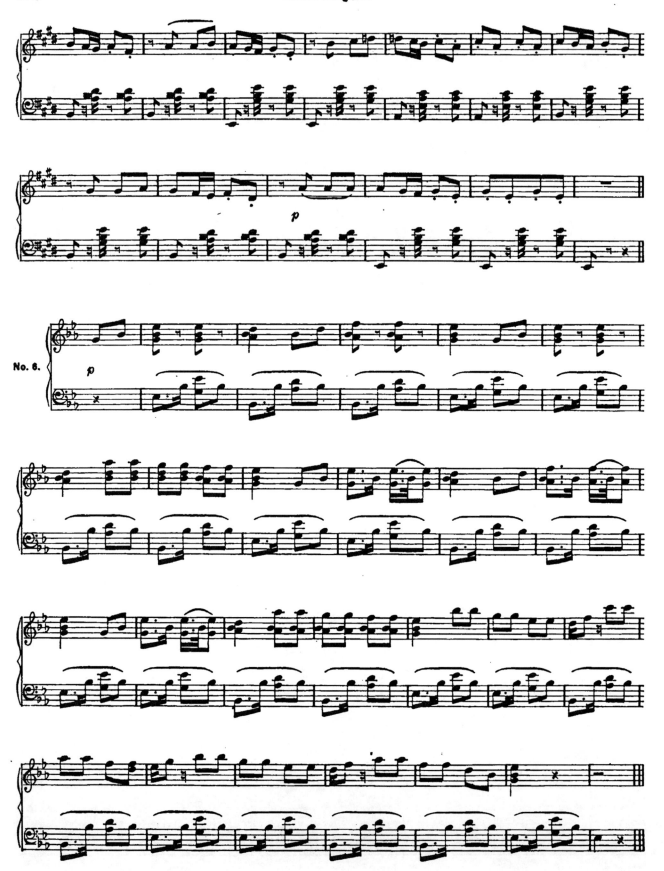

MEXICO.

"Mexicanos, al grito de guerra."

NATIONAL AIR.

J. Nunó.

MEXICO.

MOLDAVIA.

TYPICAL AIR.

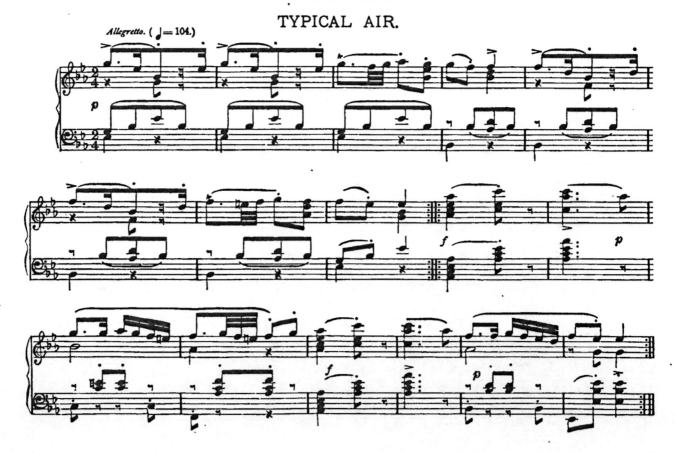

MONTENEGRO.

Onward! Onward' (Ohamo, ohamo za opga oha.)
NATIONAL AIR.

NICARAQUA.

Robert Sacasa.
PATRIOTIC AIR.

By ALESANDRO COUSIN.
Director, National Band of Nicaragua.

174

NICARAGUA.

NATIONAL AIR.

By BLAS VILLALTAR.

"This air was composed by a member of the Government Band at Managua, and having been played by that Band on occasions of state, the Government of the Republic has adopted it as the National Hymn. I received this copy from Governor Delgadillo." *Mr. Wm. A. Brown, Consul at San Juan del Norte, Nicaragua.*

NEW ZEALAND.

God Defend New Zealand.

NATIONAL ANTHEM.

Words by Thomas Bracken.

Music by John J. Woods.

"Although this air has no particular official recognition, yet it is generally understood and admitted to be the national air of the Colony as well as being the most popular."—*Extract of letter from Hon. John D. Connolly, Consul at Auckland.*

The proprietors of "The New Zealand Saturday Advertiser" having offered a prize of ten Guineas for the best musical composition to a National Hymn, written by Thomas Bracken, Esq., the appointed judges, Messrs. Zelman, Zeplin and Siede, of Melbourne, selected the Composition of John J. Woods, Esq., of Lawrence, Otago, as the best, and unanimously awarded him the prize.

NORWAY.

Sons of dear Norway. (Sonner af Norge.)

PATRIOTIC SONG.

Words by MINDING.
Translated by Thos. B. Kirby.

2.	2.
Land of great mountains, snow-peaked, cloud-capped and rugged,	*O theures Land mit den wolkigen Spitzen,*
Vales rich and fertile, and seas filled with fish! ·	*Fruchtbaren Thälern und fischreichen Seen,*
Now and for all time, thy people love thee dearly,	*Du wirst die Liebe der Deinen besitzen;*
Would die for thy sake, if 'tis thy royal wish.	*Rufst-Du, für Dich wirst du bluten uns seha.*
Dearest of mothers,	*Liebstes der Lande*
We stand as brothers,	*Stehe, zum Pfande*
Pledged to defend thee for liberty's sake.	*Ewiger Freiheit ihr Heiligthum !*
Grow, grand old nation, surpassing all others,	*Wachse so lang noch die Welle am Strande*
Until the waves on thy shores cease to break.	*Brauset, o wachse an Glück wie am Ruhm!*

ORANGE FREE STATE.

Sing, citizens, the song of Freedom. (Heft, Burgers, 't lied der vrijheid.)

NATIONAL AIR.

Words by H. A. L. HAMELBERG.
Translation by HERMANN JACOBSON.

Music by W. F. G. NICOLAI.

2.	2.
If brutal force drives us to war,	*Dwingt woest gemeld ons tot der strijd,*
Should despot in his arrogance	*Geschonden en af waardejhied*
Cause us to seize the sword,—	*Tot 't grijpen van het zwaard,.*
We'll use it with the lion's strength,	*Dan trekken w'ap mes lecumenesed*
Protect our home with vigilance,	*En aff'ren gaarne goed en bloed*
For Liberty's our Lord.	*Voor 't land, ons lief en waard.*

NUKAHIVAH ISLAND.

SONG.

PERU.

Somos libres, seamoslo siempre!

NATIONAL AIR.

CHORUS.

Somos libres, seámoslo siempre!
Y ántes niegue sus luces el sol,
Que faltemos al voto solemne
Que la Patria al Eterno elevo˙

I.

Largo tiempo el peruano oprimido
La ominosa cadena arrastró,
Condenado á una cruel servidumbre
Largo tiempo en silencio gimió!
Mas apenas el grito sagrado
¡Libertad! en sus costas se oyó,
¡La indolencia de esclavo sacude,
La humillada serviz levantó!

2.

Ya el estruendo de broncas cadenas
Que escuchamos tres siglos de horror,
De los libres al grito sagrado
Que oyó atónito el mundo, cesó.
Por do quier San Martin inflamado
Libertad, libertad pronunció,
Y meciendo su base los Andes
La enunciaron tambien á una voz!

3.

Del letargo en que estaba sumida
Lima se alza y su frente arrugó,
Al lanzar al tirano impotente
Que intentaba alargar su opresion.
A su esfuerzo saltaron los grillos,
Y los surcos que en si reparó
Le atizaron el ódio y venganza'
Que heredó de su Inca y Señor.

4.

Compatriotas, no mas verla esclava!
Si humillada tres siglos gimió!
Para siempre jurémosla libre
Manteniendo su propio esplendor.
Nuestros brazos hasta hoy desarmados
Estén siempre cebando el cañon,
Que algun dia en las playas de Iberia
Lanzará, en humo denso, terror!

PERSIA.

Salamati Shah.

NATIONAL AIR.

By A. LEMAIRE.

184   PERSIA.

PHILIPPINE ISLANDS.

TYPICAL AIRS.

"The second air in this collection, "Ang Bayuhan," and the third, "Ang Palimos," are the favorites. The words for these songs, which I have been unable to procure, are in the "Tagaloc" dialect and as they vary considerably according to the circumstances under which the song is sung, they have never been printed.

It is the custom with the natives to improvise words in "Tagaloc" for the music, as they chant it without any attempt at rhyme; the subject being generally of an amatory character. They accompany themselves with the guitar, and as good voices are by no means rare among them, one frequently hears most sweetly melodious music emanating from their rude huts at night."—*From Alex. R. Webb, Esq., Consul at Manila, Philippine Islands.*

Ang Palimos.

rall.
Ped.
Andante. Ang Cundiman.
p Doloroso.
ten.
dim.
espress.
8va
Con dolore.

PHILIPPINE ISLANDS.

PHILIPPINE ISLANDS.

PHILIPPINE ISLANDS.

PHILIPPINE ISLANDS.

POLAND.

Poland's not yet dead in slavery.

PATRIOTIC SONG.

By Sowinski.

Allegretto.

1. Po - land's not yet dead in slav - 'ry, She once more shall
1. *Jesz - cze Po - lska nie zje - ne - ta, Kie - dy my zy -*

reign; What she lost her chil - dren's brav - 'ry Soon will free a - gain! Skrzy - ne - cki* leads us on,—
je - my Co nam ob - ca prze mocznie Ta sza bla oc bie - rzemy. Jus Skrzynecki namdowodsi,

Hark! the bat - tle fray is rag - ing; Po - land shall be free! Crush all ty - ran - ny!
Jus wre wal ha sro - ga. Po - lska, wol - nasie odro - dsi bo po - lic - gem wro - ga.

2.
Polish blood's already flowing,
  But our swords are drawn.
Hope in each brave heart is glowing—
  All to fight are gone!
    Skrzynecki leads us on, &c.

3.
See the Czar's great army shatter'd,
  In its proud array!
See, his conquer'd legions scatter'd,
  Poles have gained the day!
    Shrzynecki leads us on, &c.

2.
*Jus car parwae za mices krwawy,
  Jus krew polska plynie,
Leca lud wolnej broniac sprawy,
  Zwyciesy lub zgenie.
    Jus Skrzynecki, &c.*

3.
*Wsnil sie wiec u dawnej swietnosci,
  Drogi orle bealy,
A wnet u szezesciu i wolnosci,
  Ujrzys narodcaly.
    Jus Skrzynecki, &c.*

*Skrzynecki, (pronounce Skrahe-nets-key,) a Polish officer, was intrusted by the Polish National Parliament, during the struggle of that nation for liberation from the Russian yoke, (1830–81) with the command-in-chief of the national forces. Skrzynecki gained some brilliant victories over the Russian armies (March to August, 1831), but the fruits of his successes were lost by his unaccountable hesitation in prosecuting them to the end. The suspicion that he temporised with the Russians for his own ends led the National Parliament to institute a court of inquiry into his generalship. He then resigned the chief command, after holding it for the brief period of about 8 months, during which his victories had raised the nation's hopes to the highest point.

Skrzy - ne - cki...... leads us on, Hark! the battle-fray is rag - ing, Po - land shall be free,........ Crush all ty - ran - ny!

Jus Skrzynecki namdowodsi, Jus wre wal ka sro - ga, Po - lska, wol-nasie odro - dzi bo po - lic-gem wro-ga.

PRUSSIA.

I am a Prussian. (Preussens Vaterland.)

PATRIOTIC SONG.

Music by A. NEITHARDT.

1. I am a Prus - sian! do you know my col - ors? The standard floats be - fore me black and
1. *Ich bin ein Preu - sse! Kennt ihr mei - ne Far - ben? Die Fah - ne schwebt mir weiss und schwarz vor-*
2. With lov - ing pride I for my coun - try of - fer, (Where our great Fred - 'rick's fame doth hov - er
2. *Mit Stols und Lie - be opfr' ich gern dem Lan - de, (das un - sers gro - ssen Friedrichs Ruhm um-*

white; My fa - thers' died their lib - er - ty de - fend - ing, Which doth pro - claim the col - ors mine by
an, dass für die Frei - heit mei - ne Vä - ter star - ben, das deu - ten, merkt es, mei - ne Fur - ben
round,) Un - to my foe my life I'd free - ly prof - fer, Tho' on the mar - gin of th' a - byss pro-
schwebt,) mein Preu-ssen-blut wenn es am stei - len Ran - de des Ab-grunds steht, von Fein-den kühn er-

PORTUGAL.

NATIONAL AIR.

By Henrique Müller Junior.

Upon the accession of a Sovereign to the throne of Portugal, a new national hymn is composed and adopted. The above hymn was first played on the occasion of the acclamation of Don Carlos I, on the 21st of December, 1889.

PONCA INDIANS.

LOVE SONG.

REPUBLIC OF COLOMBIA.

NATIONAL AIR.

ROUMANIA.

Soldier's Dance.

TYPICAL.

ROUMANIA.

Shepherd's Dance.

TYPICAL.

ROUMANIA.

Hora sentimentale.

ΤΥΡΙCAL.

PFALZ.

The Hunter of the Palatinate.

TYPICAL AIRS OF THE UPPER PALATINATE.

Da Capo.

ROUMANIA.

Long live the King. (Traeasca Regele.)

NATIONAL AIR.

Words by V. ALEXANDRI.

Music by ED. A.HÜBSCH, Op. 68.

In 1861 the Government of Roumania offered a prize for the best national hymn. The above hymn won the prize, and was adopted by the Roumanian army on the 22d of January, 1862.

RUSSIA.

Lord God, protect the Czar!

NATIONAL AIR.

Words by JOUKOWSKY.

Music by A. von LVOFF.

RUSSIAN WORDS.

Boshe zar ia chrani,
Sstll nyi derzhan nsd,
Zarst wui na Slawyi, na
Sla wu nam.
Zarst wui na slack wragam
Zar prawa sslawnyi,
Boshe zar ia chrani.

"This hymn was composed by Col. Alexis von Lvoff,' and dates from 1830, when by order of Nicholas it was performed in concerts and representations on the stage."—*Engel.*

faith's true pro - tect - or, Long live the Czar!

ff Chorus.

He is our guid - ing star, Great in peace and war, Our

faith's true pro - tect - - or, God save the Czar!

High the Cossack's heart is bounding.

THE COSSACK'S SONG.

J. C. Grünbaum.

1. Ho! ho! ho! ho! ho! High the Cos - sack's heart is
2. Ho! ho! ho! ho! ho! Yet the rest - less Cos - sack
3. Ho! ho! ho! ho! ho! Broth - ers, let us all be

bound - ing, When the bat - tle - call he hears. Ho! ho! ho! ho! When the wild "hur - rah" is
nev - er Long a peace - ful life can lead. Ho! ho! ho! ho! Ha! his heart is burn - ing
meet - ing, Brave and free, the foe at hand. Ho! ho! ho! ho! High our hearts to - day are

sound - ing Wel - come mu - sic to his ears! Hur - rah! Hur -
ev - er T'wards the bat - tle - field to speed! Hur - rah! Hur -
beat - ing, They to - mor - row still may stand! Hur - rah! Hur -

rah! When his steed to com - bat spring - ing On - ward strains, High in air his lance he's swing - ing, Fights and
rah! When the can - non's roar he hear - eth Nought fears he, E'en the face of death he near - eth Laughing -
rah! Let the grave be dread - ed nev - er At the end, If the foe but with us ev - er There de -

gains! High in air his lance he's swing - ing, Fights and gains! Hur - rah!......... hur - rah!......... ho!
ly, E'en the face of death he near - eth Laugh - ing - ly. Hur - rah!......... hur - rah!......... ho!
scend! If the foe but with us ev - er There de - scend! Hur - rah!......... hur - rah!......... ho!

sentations on the

RUSSIA.

The Cossack.

OLD RUSSIAN SONG OF UKRAINE.

4.
At the tables sit two men and not a word they say,
Two full inkstands there have they,
Inkstands full have they, inkstands full have they.

5.
Near them is a gentle maid, her face is young and fair,
She is standing weeping there.
She is weeping there, she is weeping there.

6.
Weep not for thy love, dear maid, for him thou'st nought to fear,
He'll not be a musketeer,
Not a musketeer, not a musketeer.

7.
Nay, he'll mount much higher, greatly honor'd now is he;
Cossack of the Don he'll be,
Cossack of the Don, of the Don he'll be.

"Ukraine, or Kharkof, is the name of a province of "Little Russia," on the banks of the Dnieper. This song refers to the enrollment of a recruit into the rank of the "Don Cossacks," who are considered to belong to the élite of the army of Russia."—*Kappey.*

SALSBURG.

Schnödahöpfl.

TYPICAL SONG.

Allegretto.

1st singer. Four maidens fair and come-ly Are much belov'd by me; How can I ev-er man-age That *each* my love shall be?
2d singer. I'll wink to one most gai-ly, Tread on the sec-ond's toe; The third I'll beckon sly-ly, The fourth a kiss I'll blow.
3d singer. The sea is full of wa-ter, The wa-ter turns to ice; That love each day grows cold-er, Is nothing new or nice.

4th singer. Be-neath the maid's win-dow Is writ-ten hard by: "Take care not to fall, youth, The win-dow is high!"

5th singer. A las-sie for lov-ing, A dog-gie for speed-ing, A ri-fle for shoot-ing, A sports-man is need-ing.

6th singer. The youths of old Salz-burg Love boast-ing and play-ing; Their wa-ges go quick-ly When debts they are pay-ing.

7th singer.

When confessing last, I said:
"Sir, I cannot catch the maid."
Said the Priest: "My son, you see,
Just the same it is with me!"

(Music ad lib.)

8th singer.

Who'll charcoal-burner marry
Must soap in pocket carry!
And rub with all their might
Before they'll see him white.

SALZBURGER RHYMES.

"Schnödahöpfl'n" form a distinct class of National Songs, belonging exclusively to the Province of Salsburg in Upper Austria. The term is untranslatable, and the meaning of it might perhaps be rendered by "witty ditty." The people of Salsburg are very fond of dancing, and a holiday mostly brings the young folks of the village together for a "Dreher." The intervals between the dances are then enlivened by the singing of Schnödahöpfl'n, *sung in rotation,* and frequently *extemporised.* Their singing is sometimes used by the young men to make their rivals in love ridiculous before the assembled maidens, and consequently leads sometimes to serious quarrels.

The essential quality of a good "Schnödahöpfl" is a broad humor, condensed into four lines. It may be mentioned that *several* collections of these little Rhymes have been made, and in one alone of these "Salsburger Volkslieder" by M. V. Süss, *one thousand* are recorded, proving the antiquity and extent of the custom.

The frequent visits of modern tourists to this beautiful province tend to obliterate these pastimes, and the author of the work mentioned above, laments the fact, that where formerly the "Dreher" and "Schnödahöpfl" were alone patronised, one could see now the Polka and Cotillon preferred. The above few examples must suffice to give a rough idea of these quatrains, the peculiarly broad and often coarsely biting humor is, however, impossible to preserve in the translation.—*Koppey, in Songs of Eastern Europe.*

SALVADOR.

Salute our country. (Saludemos la Patria.)

NATIONAL SONG.

Letra de JUAN J. CAÑAS.
Translation by E. M. TABER.

Música de J. ABERLE.

We, her chil-dren, with fond ad-o-ra-tion, Hon-or our
Sa-lu-de-mos la Pa-tria or-gu-llo-sos De hi-jos

na-tive land and fer-vent-ly, tru-ly we swear, That we pledge our lives to our
su-yos po-der-nos lla-mar............ Y ju-re-mos la vi-da a-ni-

na-tion, To her pros-per-i-ty and wel-fare, To her wel-
mo-sos Sin des-can-so á su bien con-sa-grar, Sin con-sa-

tare, her wel-fare, her wel-fare..........................
grar, con sa-grar, con sa-grar.....

FIN. SOLO.

1. Sal - va - dor in her no-ble-ness ev - - er Has made
2. Lib - er - ty is her guide and her watch - - word, A thou-

1. De la paz En la dicha su - pre - - ma Siem - pre
2. Li - ber - tad es su dogmaessu guí - - a Que mil
3. To - dos son ad - ne - ga - dos y fie - - les Al pres -

FIN.

bless-ed Peace her glo-ri-ous aim, To at - tain.......... it has been her en - deav - - or, To pre-
sand times in its sa-cred name, Has she driv - - en out audacious ty - - rants, Who......

o - ble so-ñoel Sal - va - dor Fué ob - te - - ner la sueter-no-pro-ble - - ma, con - serve - tes lo-gró de - fen : der, Yo-tras tan - - tasde audástira - ni - - a re - cha-
ti - gio del bé-lico ar - dor, Con que siem - - pre se-garonlau-re - - les De la

serve.......... it her crown.......... of fame. With a firm, strong heart, and with faith un-
sought......... to as - sail.............. its fame. Sad and stained with blood is Sal - va-dor's life

var - - lae-ssu glo - - ria ma - yor. Y con fé in-que-bran-ta - ble el ca-
zar - el o - dio - so po - der. Do - lo - ro - sa y san-grientae-ssu his -
Pa - - tria sal - van - - do el ho - nor. Res - pe - tar los de - re - chos ex -

swerv - ing, In the broad path of Pro - gress on does she press, To the des - ti - ny her val - or is
sto - ry, But yet bril - liant and loft - y as stars in the night, For her Spar - tan...... de - vo - tion was

mi - no Del pro-gre - so se afa - na en se - guir en se - guir Por lle - nar su-grandi - o - so des -
to - ria Pe - ro exel - sa y brillan - te á la vez; á la vez Ma - nan - tial de le - gí - ti - ma
tra - ños Y a - po - yar seen la rec - ta ra - zón, ra - zón Es pa - rae - lla-sin-tor - pes a -

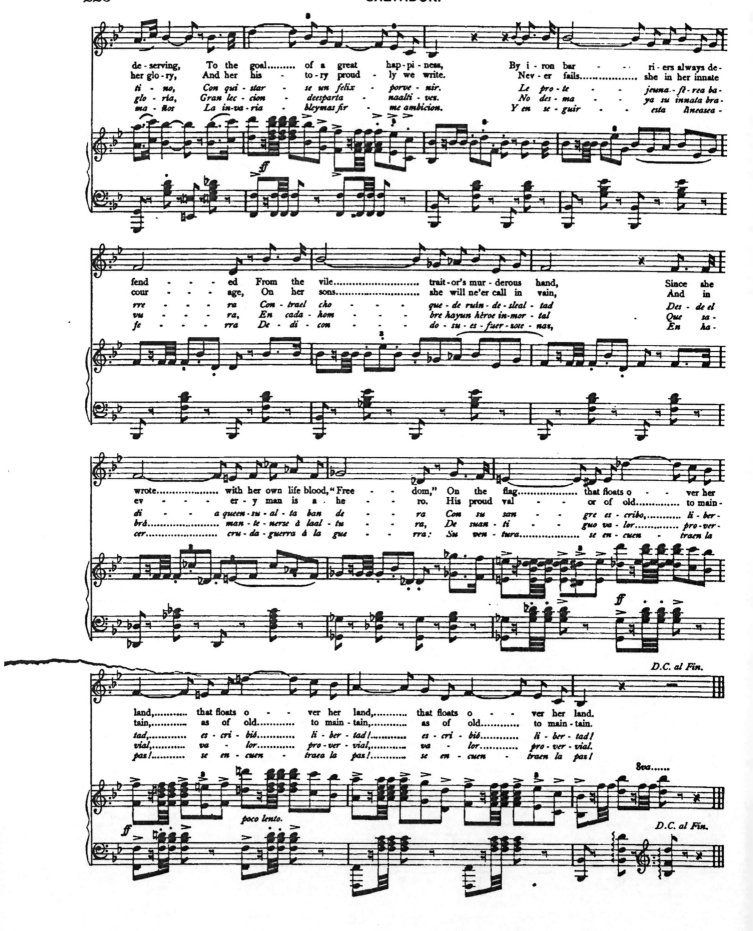

D.C. al Fin.

SAMOA.

Esia Samoa.

WAR SONG.

E - si - a Sa - moa a - pa - la nov nov fo - a foa-fe tui - le a - la a - la

po - po to ar - fe - ti a mai fi na-mo to le Vai-van fa lau - ua tai mai le ou lu.

SILESIA.

Tell me pray.

TYPICAL AIR.

Moderato.

1. Tell me pray, oh gar - d'ner mine, Are thy beds not grow - ing La - ven - der and
2. "Yes, Mam' - selle, I've all the best, In my gar - den yon - der, Will you be so
3. "Lad - die, bring the set - tle here, Bright with gold lace gleam - ing, Tir'd will be Mam' -

rose - m'ry fine, Thyme in fra - grance blow - ing? 4. "Lad - die, cull a po - sy fair,
good and rest, Ere a - way you wan - der?" 5. Then the hon - est lad - die went
selle, I fear, She would rest 'tis seem - ing." 6. Then he bound with silk - en band,

From the beds and bow - ers; Yet be sure and take great care Not to tread the flow - ers."
T'wards the gar - den slow - ly; Both his bright blue eyes were bent On the maid - en low - ly.
Myr - tles green and ro - ses; Of - fer'd there the maid his hand With the fra - grant po - sies.

SAN DOMINGO.

Quis gus ya nosvalientes.

NATIONAL AIR.

By José Reyes.

SAN MARINO.

La Sammarinese.

NATIONAL AIR.

lac - cio sde-gnan - do esser do - ma Le gran-d'a - li rac - col - se, le gran

lac - cio sde-gnan-do esser do - ma Le gran-d'a - li rac - col - se, le gran

lac - cio sde-gran - do esser do - ma Le grand'a - li rac - col - se, le gran -

d'a - li rac - colse e po - sò. Sal - - ve, Sal - ve.

d' - li rac-colse e po - sò. Sal - ve, Sal - ve.

d'a - li rac-colse e po - sò. Sal - ve, Sal - ve.

No. 2. *p* SOLI.   *con transports.*

Qui a - mor del-la ter - ra na - tì - a Al - to, im - men - so su - bli - ma ogni pet - to; Qui pie -

u - na vo - ce gri - dò, Vi - va, vi - va fu l'e - co to - nan - te, Fu la

u - na vo - ce gri - dò, Vi - va, vi - va fu l'e - co to - nan - te, Fu la

Vi - va, vi - va fu l'e - co to - nan - te, Fu la

vo - ce so - len - ne dei mil - le; O - gni sguardo met - te - va fa - vil - le O - gni de - stra un acciaro snu -

vo - ce so - len - ne dei mil - le; O - gni sguardo met - te - va fa - vil - le O - gni de - stra un acciaro snu -

vo - ce so - len - ne dei mil - le; O - gni sguardo met - te - va fa - vil - le O - gni de - stra un acciaro snu -

dò! O - gni de - stra un acciaro snu - dò! Spar - ve il nem - bo! ma du - ra quel

dò! O - gni de - stra un acciaro snu - dò! Spar - ve il nem - bo! ma du - ra quel

dò! O - gni de - stra un acciaro snu - dò!

No. 8. *Marcate.*

tù de' vo-stri avi si muor." Ma al sol lam-po dell' e - gi-da e-ter - na Di giu-

tù de' vo-stri avi si muor." Ma al sol lam-po dell' e - gi-da e-ter - na Di giu-

Marcate.

sti - zia, che è forza di Di - o, Ca - - - de in-fran-to ne - mi-co de-si - - - o, cade in-fran - to

sti - zia, che è forza di Di - o, Ca - - - de in-fran-to ne - mi-co de-si - - - o, cade in-fran - to

Ca - - - de in-fran-to ne - mi-co de-si - - - o, cade in-fran - to

f

Ed il - le - sa la pa - tri - a sta: Sem - pre, sem - pre il -

Ed il - le - sa la pa - tri - a sta: Sem - pre, sem - pre il -

Ed il - le - sa la pa - tri - a sta: Sem - pre, sem - pre il -

Con giubilo.

squillo.

SAVOY.

TYPICAL AIR.

SIAM.

TYPICAL AIR.

236

SCHLESWIG HOLSTEIN.

Schleswig-Holstein Meerumschlungen.

PATRIOTIC AIR.

C. G. BELLMAN.

This song was composed in 1844, and served greatly to arouse the sense of patriotism in Germany, in face of the fact that two beautiful German provinces were suffering under the tyranny of Denmark. The song again revived in 1864, when Austria, in connection with Prussia, wrested the two States from Denmark.

SIAM.

NATIONAL AIR.

This air was given the compiler by the Siamese Embassy on the occasion of their visit to this country some years since.

SCOTLAND.

Scots, wha hae wi' Wallace bled!

PATRIOTIC SONG.

Words by ROBERT BURNS.
(Born 1759, died 1796.)

Air—"HEY TUTTI TAITTI."

1. Scots, wha hae wi' Wal-lace bled, Scots, wham Bruce has af-ten led,

Wel-come to your go-ry bed, Or to vic-to-rie! Now's the day an' now's the hour.

See the front of bat-tle lour; See ap-proach proud Ed-ward's pow'r, Chains and sla-ve-rie!

2.
Wha would be a traitor knave?
Wha would fill a coward's grave?
Wha sae base as be a slave?
    Let him turn an' flee!
Wha, for Scotland's king an' law,
Freedom's sword would strongly draw,
Freeman stand, and freeman fa',
    Let him on wi' me!

3.
By oppression's woes an' pains,
By your sons in servile chains,
We will drain our dearest veins,
    But they shall be free.
Lay the proud usurpers low!
Tyrants fall in every foe!
Liberty's in every blow!
    Let us do or dee!

"There is a tradition which I have met with in many places in Scotland, that it ('Hey tuttie taittie'), was Robert Bruce's march at the battle of Bannockburn. This thought, in my solitary wanderings, warmed me to a pitch of enthusiasm on the theme of liberty and independence, which I threw into a kind of Scottish ode, fitted to the air, that one might suppose to be the gallant royal Scot's address to his heroic followers on that eventful day. So may God defend the cause of truth and liberty as he did that day! Amen."—*Burns' letters to Thomson.*

SCOTLAND.

Bonnie Dundee.

PATRIOTIC SONG.

Sir Walter Scott.

Allegretto.

1. To the Lords of Con - ven - tion 'twas
2. Dun - dee he is mount - ed, he

Claverhouse spoke : Ere the King's crown go down there are crowns to be broke, Then each cavalier who loves honour and me, Let him follow the bonnets of
rides up the street, The bells they ring backward, the drums they are beat, But the provost (douce man) said, " Just e'en let it be, For the toun is weel rid o' that

Bonnie Dundee. Come fill up my cup, come fill up my can, Come saddle my horses, and call out my men; Un - hook the west port, and
de'il o' Dundee. Come fill up my cup, come fill up my can, Come saddle my horses, and call out my men; Un - hook the west port, and

let us gae free, For its up wi' the bonnets of Bonnie Dundee.

3.
There are hills beyond Pentland, and lands beyond Forth,
Be there lords in the south, there are chiefs in the north;
There are brave Duinnewassels three thousand times three,
Will cry, " Hey for the bonnets o' Bonnie Dundee."
Come fill up my cup, etc.

4.
Then awa' to the hills, to the lea, to the rocks,
Ere I own a usurper I'll crouch with the fox;
And tremble, false whigs, in the midst o' your glee
Ye hae no seen the last o' my bonnets and me.
Come fill up my cup, etc.

SCOTLAND.

Blue bonnets over the border.
PATRIOTIC SONG.

Sir Walter Scott.

March! march! Ett-rick and Te-viot-dale, Why, my lads, din-na ye march for-ward in or-der?

March! march! Esk-dale and Lid-des-dale, All the blue bon-nets are o-ver the bor-der.

Ma-ny a ban-ner spread, flut-ters a-bove your head, Ma-ny a crest that is fa-mous in sto-ry:

Mount and make read-y then, sons of the moun-tain glen, Fight for your Queen and the old Scot-tish glo-ry.

Come from the hills where your hirsels are grazing,
Come from the glen of the buck and the roe;
Come to the crag where the beacon is blazing,
Come with the buckler, the lance, and the bow.
Trumpets are sounding, war steeds are bounding,
Stand to your arms, and march in good order;
England shall many a day tell of the bloody fray,
When the blue bonnets came over the border.
March, march, Ettrick and Teviotdale, etc.

SERVIA.
God in His Goodness.
NATIONAL AIR.

Composed by Davorin Jenko.

ST. PAUL DE LOANDO.
TYPICAL AIR.

No. 1.

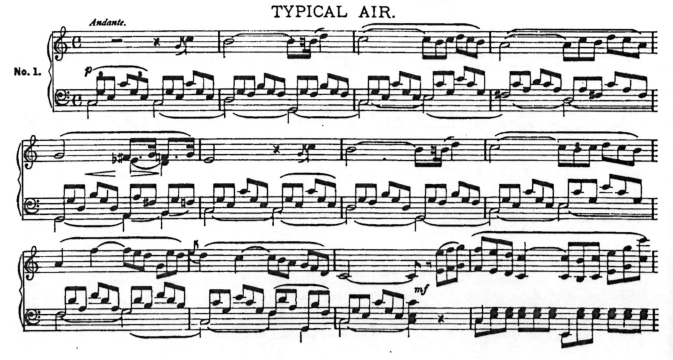

SERVIA.

Rise, Servians.

PATRIOTIC SONG.

1. Ser - via, peaceful land of flow'rs, Home of vines and leaf - y bow'rs, Thou, the Danube's gentle daughter, Rise, pre-pare for slaughter!
2. Free are Sàv and Duna's waves, Shall then we be Turkish slaves? Like Stefàn* so fam'd in sto - ry, We will lead to glo - ry!

Foes are near, will Ser - via cow - er? Rise, and strike for freedom's dow - er! Tho' no state - ly tow'rs have we
Foes are near, will Ser - via cow - er? Rise, and strike for freedom's dow - er! Bal - kan vales, Mo - ra - vian land,

Yet our land is fair and free! } Servians, quit the plough and teth - er, One and all we'll fight to - geth - er! We will fight to-
Free shall be from ty - rant's hand! }

geth - er, Foes are near, will Ser - via cow - er? Rise, and strike for free - dom's dow - - er!

"Servian Songs are very melodious, and many have the peculiarity of ending a note above the keynote, which is especially prominent in the National Song "Rise Servians," the music of which has as powerful an effect upon the natives as the Marseillaise has upon the French. Although the number of Servian songs is very great, yet comparatively little progress has been made in collecting them, and by far the greater number are as yet preserved in the primitive way of tradition. What Owen Meredith says of Servian poetry may justly be applied to the native melodies: "Such flowers as grow here may be merely mountain weeds, but the dew of the morning is on them.""—*Songs of Eastern Europe.*

*Stefan Nemanga, who about 1165 liberated his country from the yoke of the Byzantine Empire, and founded the Servian Kingdom. His Dynasty ruled over the state for some centuries, and considerably enlarged its boundaries.

SLAVONIA.

Is on earth another love like mine.

TYPICAL SONG.

1. Is on earth an - oth - er love like mine, which nev - er joy is know -
2. Is on earth an - oth - er maid so fair as thou, so heart - less ev -

ing? Is on earth an - oth - er heart like mine, with se - cret sor - row glow -
er? Ah, thy glance dis - dain - ful kills me, vain is ev - 'ry wild en - deav -

ing. Ah! love for thee, thee on - ly, I weep for - ev - er lone - ly.
our My love in words to fash - ion, To move thee to com - pas - sion!

Fain would I be tell - ing, All the sor - row swell - ing, My lone - ly breast.
Ah! wouldst thou be spurn - ing, If thou knew how burn - ing With love's my breast?

SPAIN.

Hymno de Riego.

NATIONAL AIR.

By HUERTA.

1. Serenely and with valor
   Come raise your manly voices;
   For all our land rejoices
   In praises of the king.
   With patriotic fervor—
   Devoted to our nation—
   We'll die for her salvation,
   Her glories let us sing.

CHORUS.—Then soldiers patriotic,
   The nation looks to you
   To show by deeds of valor,
   That to her cause you're true.

2. The sleeping sword awaken!
   By words and deed we're plighted
   To save the slave affrighted,
   And make our brother free.
   Though in the combat gory
   A comrade brave should perish,
   One thought we'll always cherish,
   He died for liberty.—Chorus.

3. The thunder of the cannon,
   The bugle of the battle,
   Together with the rattle
   Of musketry is rife.
   The God of war admires
   The man who knows no danger,
   Whose heart to fear's a stranger,
   And is ready for the strife.—Chorus.

1. Serenos alegres,
   Valientes pesados
   Centemos soldados
   El himno alalid,
   De nuestros acentos,
   El orbe se admire,
   Yen nosotros mire
   Los hijos del cid.

CHORUS.—Soldados la patria
   Nos llama a la lid,
   Juremos por ella
   Vencer o morir.

2. Blandamos el yerro
   Del timido esclavo
   Del fuerte del bravo
   La faz no saber.
   Sus huestes cual humo
   Vereis disipadas
   Y á nuestras espadas
   Fugaces correr.—Chorus.

3. La trompa guerrera
   Sus ecos da a' viento
   Horror a'l sediento
   Ya ruge a' canon.
   Y a Marte sanudo
   La audacia provoca
   Y el ingrato invoca
   De nuestra nacion.—Chorus.

STYRIA.

The lofty mountains rich in ore.

TYPICAL SONG.

1. The lofty mountains rich in ore, Whose peaks are bound with ice-crowns hoar. A-round whose rocks dark for-ests loom, Where deep in shade fair ro-ses bloom. Tra la la la, tra la la la la la, tra la la la, tra la la la la la, tra la la la, tra la la la la la, tra la la la, tra la la la.

2. Sweet peace-ful homes rich vine leaves hide, Bright foliage clothes the soft hill-side. The pur-ple grapes, the peach-es red, The sun-light bright in heav'n o'er-head. Tra la la la,

3.
The brooks are clear, the harvests gold,
The women fair, the warriors bold,
The dear home's faithful mighty band,
My golden verdant Styrian land!
Tra la la la, &c.

4.
The ringing songs so glad and free,
From every breast burst merrily,
Resound in heaven's azure height,
Of verdant Styria fresh and bright.
Tra la la la, &c.

SWITZERLAND.

Herdsman's Song.

TYPICAL SONG.

Moderato.

To Swiss, in stran - ger's land sing ne'er His moun - tain dit - ties

fresh and fair, Or tear - drops thou'lt see fall - ing; His heart with pain Will long in vain

For all the strain's re - call - ing! A li du - li bi - la ho, la da - li bi - la ho, la

da - li bi - la ho, la da - li bi - la ho, ja bo li ho la ho ja ho!

"RANZ DE VACHES,"—(French.) "KUHREIHEN," or "KUHREIGEN,"—(German.)

"These melodies have in course of time considerably departed from their original form, which was so simple, that the Alpine shepherds could perform them on a cow-horn, the powerful notes of which produce an indescribably beautiful effect, by the many echoes raised in the valleys around. The influence of the "Kuhreihen" upon a Swiss native, when living far away from his beloved home was proverbially powerful, frequently producing home-sickness.

When Swiss mercenary legions were serving in the Netherlands and in France, the accidental hearing of one of those strains led to frequent desertion, in consequence of which the penalty of death was decreed upon any one who sang or performed the "Kuhreihen" within hearing of the Swiss troops.—*Songs of Eastern Europe.*

SWITZERLAND.
Departure for the Alps in spring.
TYPICAL SONG.

"Jodel, (pronounce Yodel,) a refrain to the songs originating in the Alpine regions of the Tyrol, Styria and Switzerland. The compass of these melodies is often very extensive, ranging from [notation] to [notation] The natives of the Alps are mostly possessed of fresh and powerful voices, and the men cultivate with special care a pure *falsetto*. The rule of the best vocal training, to conceal the "break" between chest and head notes, is in Jodeling reversed. The falsetto is practiced as a distinct register from the chest notes, and the break is made as prominent as possible, by a peculiar jerk from the lower to the higher notes.

[notation]

Chest. falsetto. ch. f. ch. f....ch. f. ch. f. ch. ...f... ch. f.

It is impossible to convey an idea of the charm of the beautiful melodies, which have an undeniable right to rank with the best of national songs, or what the German more correctly call Volkslieder.

The syllables used are a sort of do, re, mi, sol, and vary according to the singer; it must, however, be remembered that the pronunciation of the vowels must be according to the *German* alphabet."—*Songs of Eastern Europe*.

go - ing! Ha! our time of free-dom's nigh, Brac - ing air a - waits on high; T'wards the Alps we

hie. A ho al - li ho, al - li ho - u, ho - u ho ul - li lui al - li ho - u, ho - u

hol - li dul - li, hul - li. dul - li ho - u! The bird sings its lay, The lad - dies are

gay, Hur - rah! they are cry - ing, To ver - dant meads hie - ing, The maids sing all

day:— al - li ho al - li, al - li ho a u, ju al - li o, hol - li ol - li, al - li ho ul - la ha la

ho ja, la do u al-li o ho ja ho la du-a ho — u

Lively.

Ho-la! let us call, Come great, and come small, The heights we'll be

gain-ing, Where free-dom is reign-ing, Sing gai-ly then all:—La ho-

-li, al-li ho-li o a lo — lo ho — lo ho-la jo — la do-a, lo-di

ho-la, ho — la ho-jo al-li ho-a la ho li-a ho — u.

SWITZERLAND.

Song of the shepherds.

TYPICAL SONG OF THE CANTON BERNE.

Youth. My love is ve - ry dis - tant, She's on the plain be - low, My shoes, were I to
Maiden. "Thy shoes they need not suf - fer, For slip - pers thou canst wear, If *they* wear out with
Youth. I nev - er like on week-days, To - wards the plain to rove, There's hol - i - day on
Maiden. My love the horn blows fine - ly, All tunes he well doth know, He plays them ev - 'ry

walk there, Would suf - fer well I know. *Youth.* My love drives o'er the path - way, Her
walk - ing, Put on an - oth - er pair! *Maiden.* Ah! if when I am milk - ing, The
Sun - day, When I can join my love! *Youth.* The cow we'll soon be sell - ing, Yet the
morn - ing, When I to milk - ing go!

no - ble herds of kine, When I can't see them pass - ing, Then home - sick I re - pine!
cow stands wrong for - sooth, I sim - ply push her from me, And chat - ter with the youth!
calf we'll leave be - hind. No mat - ter *when* they're milk - ing, The maids I al - ways find!

SPAIN.

The Royal March.

SYRIA.

TYPICAL AIR,

"The above air, it will be observed, is written backwards, conforming to the Arabic—that is from right to left, and not as with us from left to right. I have failed to discover any original words to it, or its particular name. Perhaps it never had either."—*Henry Gillman, Esq., Consul at Jerusalem.*

TURKEY.

Our God, our God, save to us our Sultan.

A NATIONAL AIR.

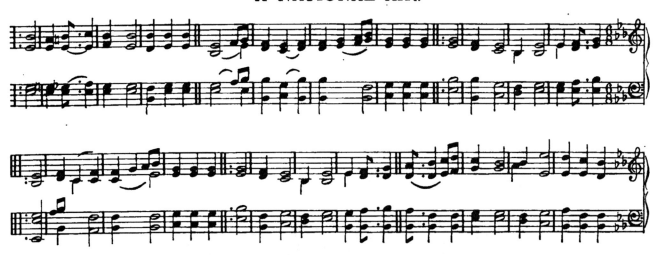

FREE TRANSLATION :— Our God, our God, save to us our Sultan,
Abd El Hamid El Ghazi, in triumph and happiness;
Save him, O God, forever, and destroy all his enemies.
Preserve him, fortified forever, in glory and happiness.
Open to him the easy way, and preserve him in the fundamental religion;
And give him full power to govern us with justice.
Preserve him to us in wisdom, and we will follow him.
Preserve him in this world in prosperity, power, and riches.
His act is highly to be honored for continuing to nominate the best of his representatives, as
Rachad Pacha, our Governor, the capable and good manager.
O God, save him to us with his wisdom;
Preserve him, forever living in honor, and keep him for us.
And the prayer continually to our Prophet is that he incline him to ameliorate our state.

"The above air is of Syrian origin. Some years ago, a Syrian gentleman named Marūn En-Nagguash wrote words to be sung to it. They are in the nature of a hymn or prayer for the late Sultan. After his death the names of the present Sultan and the present Governor of Palestine were substituted."—*Henry Gillman, Esq., Consul at Jerusalem.*

TRAMAN ISLAND.

TYPICAL AIR.

WALDECK.

PATRIOTIC AIR.

TRANSVAAL, or SOUTH-AFRICAN REPUBLIC.

The Fourcolor.

NATIONAL AIR.

TURKEY.

Dechme Daghi.

TYPICAL AIR,

TURKEY.

TRANSVAAL, or SOUTH-AFRICAN REPUBLIC.

The Fourcolor.

PATRIOTIC AIR.

The Fourcolor.

PATRIOTIC AIR,

TRIESTE.

All Hail, San Giusto. (Viva San Giusto.)

NATIONAL SONG.

By C. Sinico.

258

TRIESTE.

FINE.

TURKEY.

Hamidie.

IMPERIAL AIR

OF

SULTAN ABDUL HAMED KHAN II.

Words by HADJI EMIN BEY.   Music by NEDGIB PACHA.

Although a great Empire, Turkey has no National Hymns, the Hymns are called the Sultan's Hymn, or Prayer,—and, as a gentleman of high Turkish rank states, "They are always buried with the Sultan."

I.

Oh! universal benefactor, sovereign of sovereigns!
Glory of the throne of the Ottoman monarchy,
Under your Imperial auspices the country is prospering,
Reign always, and be always happy.
Oh! my august sovereign Sultan Hamid!

Long live our monarch with his glory;
Long live our sovereign with his grandeur!

I.

O! bienfaiteur universel, souverain des souverains;
Gloire du trône de la monarchie Ottomane,
Sous vos auspices impériales le pays prospère.
Règnes longtemps, soyez toujours heureux
O! mon auguste souverain Sultan Hamid;

Vive notre monarque avec sa gloire;
Vive notre souverain avec sa grandeur.

VANCOUVER INDIANS.

Waich ee.

SONG.

TURKEY.

MODERN PATRIOTIC WAR MARCH.

(A song of deeds of arms and valor,
by NEDGIB PACHA, chief of the Sultan's band.)

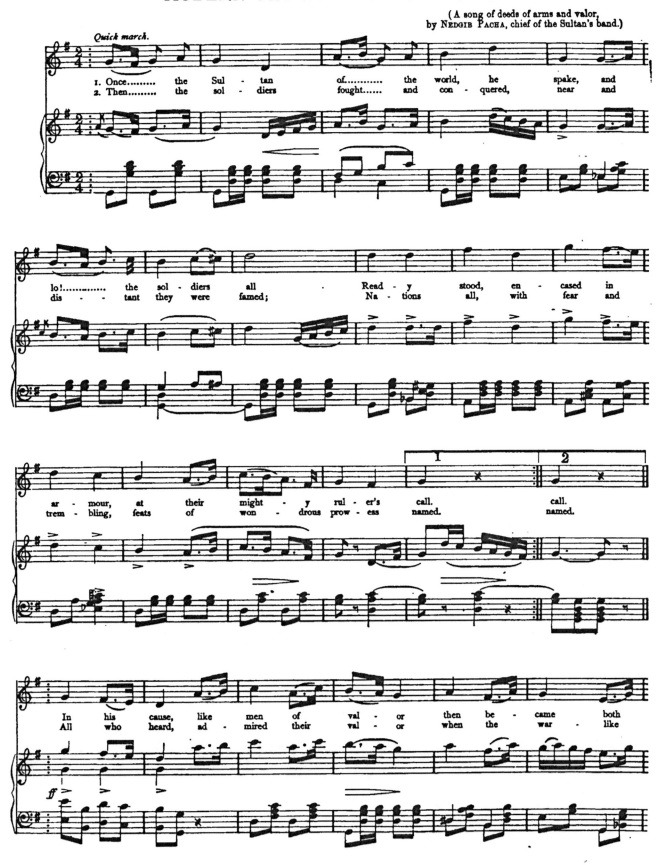

1. Once.......... the Sul - tan of............ the world, he spake, and lo!.............. the sol - diers all . Read - y stood, en - cased in ar - mour, at their might - y rul - er's call. In his cause, like men of val - or then be - came both

2. Then.......... the sol - diers fought...... and con - quered, near and dis - - tant they were famed; Na - tions all, with fear and trem - bling, feats of won - drous prow - ess named. All who heard, ad - mired their val - or when the war - like

young and old,   In his cause, like men of val - or, then be - came both
deeds were told,   All who heard, ad - mired their val - or, when the war - like

young and old.—   God will help us, save the Sul - tan, 'neath whose sha - dow
deeds were told.— God will help us, save the Sul - tan, 'neath whose sha - dow

all are bold!
all are bold!

3.

Mighty was th' Imperial army, ever mightier it grew,
North and south, and east and west, all lands the name of Turkey knew!
‖: Honored high was then our ruler, he unbounded sway did hold, :‖
Lord, oh help us save the Sultan, 'neath whose shadow *all* our bold!

4.

Turks, ha! saved with God's assistance, shall our noble monarch be,
He'll Constantinople's children make again both rich and free!
‖: Rich and happy he will make them, like in glorious days of old, :‖
Lord, oh help us save the Sultan, 'neath whose shadow *all* are bold!

TURKEY.

Charki. Indjitmé beni chouhi chinèm guel sitéminlé.

TYPICAL AIR.

Ethem Bey.

TYROL.

Andreas Hofer.

NATIONAL SONG.

Words by J. Mosen. (1831.)

Moderato.

1. In Man-tu-a in fet-ters, The faith-ful Ho-fer lay, In
1. Zu Man-tu-a in Ban-den der treu-e Ho-fer war, in
2. With hands fast tied be-hind him, He marched with stead-y pace; With
2. Die Hän-de auf dem Rü-cken, An-dre-as Ho-fer ging mit

Man-tu-a the hos-tile horde Took his brave life a-way. With grief his com-rade's
Man-tu-a zum To-de führt' ihn der Fein-de Schaar. Es blu-te-te der
cour-age still un-flinch-ing To meet death face to face. From I-sel-berg he
ru-hig fe-sten Schrit-ten: ihm schien der Tod ge-ring: der Tod, den es so

tears now flow, All Ger-ma-ny is plunged in woe, And mourned the lov-ing band,...... Throughout his Ty-rol
Brü-der Herz, ganz Deutschland, ach! in Gram und Schmerz, mit ihm das Land Ty-rol,...... mit ihm das Land Ty-
oft had sent That wing-ed death to which he went. In his own Ty-rol land,...... In his own Ty-rol
man-ches Mal vom I-sel-berg ge-schickt in's Thal, im heil'-gen Land Ty-rol,......... im heil'-gen Land Ty-

land. And mourned the lov-ing band,...... Through-out his Ty-rol land.
rol, mit ihm das Land Ty-rol,......... mit ihm das Land Ty-rol.
land. In his own Ty-rol land,...... In his own Ty-rol land.
rol, im heil'-gen Land Ty-rol,.......... im heil'-gen Land Ty-rol.

*Surnamed, the "Tell of the Tyrol," a patriot, b. 1767, d. 1810, at the head of 18,000 peasants, defeated 25,000 French troops. The Tyrolese rejoiced in a short interval of freedom, but were again invaded by the French, when Hofer was betrayed into their hands by a villain, and after a mock trial shot by them as described.—M. X. Hayes.

3.

From dungeon bars of iron
He saw the faithful bands
Of comrades, who in prison
Stretched forth their friendly hands.
Then cried he out, "God be with you,
And our betrayed Germania, too,
And with our Tyrol land,
And with our Tyrol land!"

4.

The drummer now no longer
His deathful drum doth beat,
As Andreas Hofer marches
Beneath the gloomy gate.
Altho' in fetters he is free,
Upon the bastion firm is he,
The man of Tyrol land,
The man of Tyrol land!

5.

They fain would make the hero
Kneel humbly down to die:
"Not so!" he cried, "upright I lived,
And upright will I die!
Erect I'll stand within this trench
And cry, Long live my Emp'ror Franz!
Heav'n guard my Tyrol land,
Heav'n guard my Tyrol land!"

5.

He gave th' ignoble bandage
Unto the corp'ral there;
Then offered up to God above
A short and fervent pray'r.
He cried, "Be sure ye aim aright!
Now fire! Ah! false your bullets' flight!
Adieu, my Tyrol land,
Adieu, my Tyrol land!"

3.

Doch als aus Kerkergittern
Im festen Mantua
Die treuen Waffenbrüder
Die Händ' er strecken sah,
Da rief er aus: "Gott sei mit Euch,
Mit dem verrathnen deutschen Reich
Und mit dem Land Tyrol,
Und mit dem Land Tyrol!"

4.

Dem Tambour will der Wirbel
Nicht unter'm Schlägel vor,
Als nun Andreas Hofer
Schritt durch das finstre Thor.
Andreas, noch in Banden frei,
Dort stand er fest auf der Bastei,
Der Mann vom Land Tyrol,
Der Mann vom Land Tyrol!

5.

Dort soll er niederknieen;
Er sprach: "Das thu' ich nit!
Will sterben, wie ich stehe,
Will sterben, wie ich stritt;
So, wie ich steh' auf dieser Schanz';
Es leb' mein guter Kaiser Frans,
Mit ihm sein Land Tyrol,
Mit ihm sein Land Tyrol!"

6.

Und von der Hand die Binde
Nimmt ihm der Korporal;
Andreas Hofer betet
Allhier zum letzten Mal;
Dann ruft er: "Nun, so trefft mich recht!
Gebt Feuer!—Ach, wie schiesst ihr schlecht!
Ade, mein Land Tyrol,
Ade, mein Land Tyrol!"

MARIANNA ISLAND.

TYPICAL AIR.

UNITED STATES OF BRAZIL.

Hymn of the Proclamation of the Republic. (Hymno da Proclamacao da Republica.)

NATIONAL AIR.

Poesia de MEDEIROS E ALBUQUERQUE.

Musica de LEOPOLDO MIGUEZ.

Canto.

May the glo - ri - ous sun shed a flood of light O'er Bra - zil, with its hal - lowed sod......... Des - pots
Seja um pal - lio de lus des - do - bra - do sob a larga am - pli - dao d'es - tes chus......... es - te

nev - er a - gain will our land affright—Never more will we groan 'neath the rod. Then with hymns of glo - ry re -
can - to rebel, que o Pa - sa - do vem re - mir dos mais tor - pes la - beus! Se ja um hym - no de glo - ria que

Soon after the proclamation of the Republic of the United States of Brazil, the Minister of the Interior, ordered a competition among the native composers, for a national hymn. The above hymn was declared the successful one, and became, in January last, the hymn of the Republic.

2.

The eyes of the Day-God ne'er more will see
  The slave, in his chains, pine and die;
We are brothers who'd die for our liberty.
  Tyrants all! we your powers defy.
All are free in our glorious nation,
  In the future united are we,
While our flag waves, with wild exultation,
  We will sing of our land of the free.—Liberty, &c.

3.

From the Ypiranga, hark! 'tis the cry sublime
  Of Faith and of Hope for our land.
Come, arise! oh, Brazil, 'tis the holy time,
  Forward, all, 'tis your country's command.
From thy minds the royal purple banish,
  And in glory advance to the fore;
Then, Brazil, all thy foemen will vanish,
  And triumphant thou'lt be evermore.—Liberty, &c.

2.

*Nós nem cremos que escravos outr' ora
tenha havido em tão nobre paiz.
Hoje o rubro lampejo da aurora
acha irmãos, não tyrannos hostis.
Somos todos iguaes! Ao futuro
saberemos, unidos, levar
nosso augusto estandarte que, puro,
brilha, ovante, da Patria no altar!—Liberdade, &c.*

3.

*Do Ypiranga é preciso que o brado
seja um grito soberbo de fé!
Que o Brazil surja emfim libertado
sobre as púrpuras regias de pé!
Eia, pois, Brazileiros, avante!
Verdes louros colhamos louçãos!
Seja o nosso paiz, triumphante,
livre terra de livres irmãos!—Liberdade, &c.*

URUGUAY.

NATIONAL AIR.

By D. I. DEBALLI.

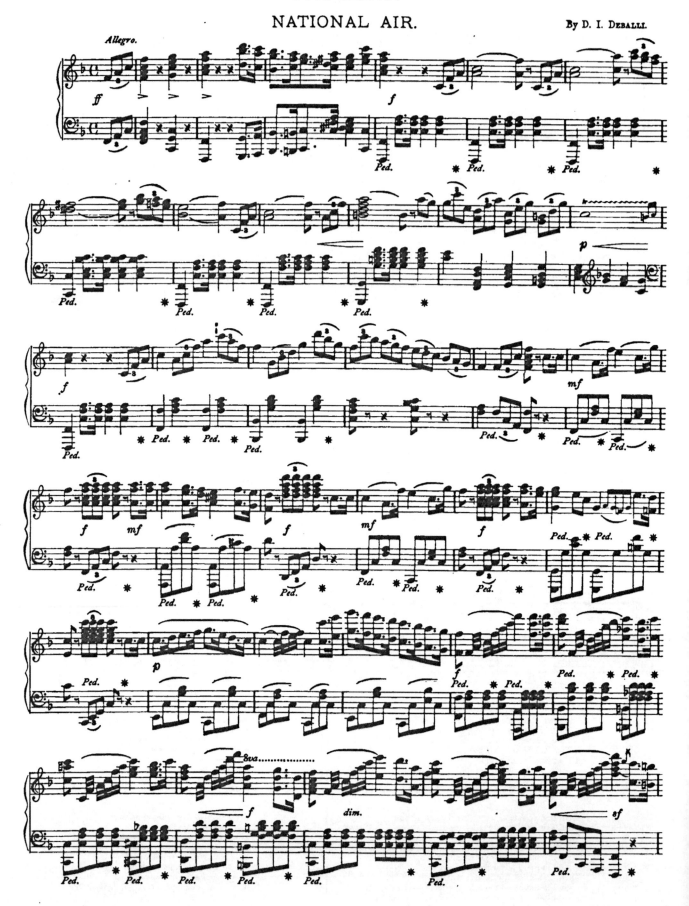

URUGUAY.

Himno Nacional de la Republica Oriental del Uruguay.

D. I. Deballi.

1.
Libertad, Libertad, Orientales,
　Este grito a la Patria salvò,
Que sus bravos en fieras batallas
　De entusiasmo sublime inflamò,
De este don sacrosanto la gloria
　Merecimos　Tiranos, temblad!
Libertad en la lid clamaremos
　Y muriendo tambien libertad!

2.
Orientales, mirad la bandera
　De heroismo fulgente crisol
Nuestras lanzas defienden su brillo
　Nadie insulte la imagen del Sol!
De los fueros civiles el goce
　Sostengamos, y el codigo fiel
Veneremos inmune, y glorioso,
　Como el arca sagrada Israel.

3.
De las leyes al numen juremos
　Igualdad, patriotismo, y union.
Inmolando en sus aras divinas
　Ciegos odios y negra ambicion,
Y hallaran los que fieros insulten
　La grandeza del pueblo Oriental,
Si enemigos, la lanza de Marte,
　Si tiranos, de Bruto el puñal.

Coro.
Orientales, la Patria ó la tumba!
　Libertad, o con gloria morir!
Es el vóto que el alma pronuncia
　Y que heroicos sabremos cumplir.

WESTPHALIA.

Es stehen drei Sterne am Himmel.

TYPICAL AIR.

VENEZUELA.

Glory to the brave people. (Gloria al bravo pueblo.)

NATIONAL AIR.

Words by VICENTE SÁLIAS.
Translation by WINFIELD S. BIRD.

Music by JOSÈ SANDAETA, (1810–1811).

1. Glo - ry to the brave men, so firm, just and true, Who broke the bonds of ty - rants and gave us free - dom too,
1. Gloria al bra - vo pue - blo que el yu - go lan - zó, La lei res - pe - tan - do la vir - tud y ho - nor,

too, Glo - ry to the brave men, so firm, just and true, Who broke the bonds of tyrants and
nor, Gloria al bra - vo pue - blo que el yu - go lan - zó La lei res - pe - tan - do

From 1810 to 1811 there existed in Caracas a League composed of notable persons called the " Patriotic Society," that labored for the independence of Venezuela.
In one of its sessions, the members full of happiness and rejoicing at the prospect of the early realization of their hopes, resolved to compose a hymn to be played and
sung upon the occasion of their triumphs. Thus the following hymn originated. The words were composed by the poet Vicente Sálias and the music was arranged by
the professor José Sandaeta, both members of said society. Since then the hymn has become one of the most popular songs in Venezuela, until, in 1881, the Government,
by Executive Decree, declared it to be the National Hymn.

long had scourged the coun - try, trem - bled with fear, That long had scourged the coun - try, trem - bled with fear.
El vil e - go - is - mo que otra vez triun - fó, el vil e - go - is - mo que otra vez triun - fó.

2.

‖: Down with the oppressor! shout long, loud huzzas;
In union, brave hearts, is the strength of our cause. :‖
    Refrain —Beneath the weight, &c.
And from the empyrean, the God of battles sent
A grand inspiration, the patriot's aliment.

3.

‖: Cemented in bonds, by Heaven's decree,
Our country is one and America is free! :‖
    Refrain —Beneath the weight, &c.
And, if the despot's voice be ever heard again,
Remember Caracas and strike with might and main.

2.

‖: *Gritámos con brio, muera la opresion,*
Compatriotas fieles, la fuersa es la union; :‖
    Refrain :—*Abajo cadenas, &c.*
Y desde el empireo el Supremo Autor
Un sublime aliento al pueblo infundió.

3.

‖: *Unida con lazos que el cielo formó*
La América toda existe ed nacion. :‖
    Refrain —*Abajo cadenas, &c.*
Y si el despotismo levanta la vox
Seguid el ejemplo que Carácas dió.

SWEDEN.

Our Swedish feelings. (Ur Svenska hjertans.)

NATIONAL AIR.

Our Swed - ish feel - ings for our king, In voi - ces pa - tri - ot - ic sing, God
Ur Svens - ka hjer - tans djup en gång en sam - fäld och en en - kel sång, som

bless our land and King. In cheer - ful - ness and sweet con - tent, In hap - pi - ness our
går till Kun - gen fram. Var ho - nom tro - fast och hans ätt, gör kro - nan på hans

lives are spent, So sing with voi - ces el - o - quent, God bless our land and King!
hjes - sa lätt, och all din tro till ho - nom sätt, du folk af frej - dad stam!

WALES.

Men of Harlech. (Rhyfelgyrch gwyr Harlech.)

PATRIOTIC SONG.

English words by JOHN OXENFORD.

ff *Molto animato.*

Men of Har - lech, march to glo - ry, Vic - to - ry is hov - 'ring o'er ye, Bright - eyed free - dom
We le goel - certh wen yn fflam - io, A thaf - od - au tân yn bloedd - io, Ar i'r dew - rion

stands be - fore ye, Hear ye not her call? At your sloth she seems to won - der,
ddod i da - ro, Un - waith et o'n un: Gan fan - llef - au ty - wys - og - ion,

8va..............................

Rend the slug - gish bonds a - sun - der, Let the war cry's deaf - 'ning thun - der, Ev - 'ry foe ap - pal.
Llais gel - yn - ion, trust arf - og - ion, A char - lam - iad y march - og - ion, Craig ar graig a gryn!

8va..............................

"*Harlech Castle* stands on a lofty rock upon the sea-shore of Merionethshire. The original tower called "*Twr Bronwen,*" is said to have been built in the sixth century; it afterwards received the name of *Caer Colwyn,* and eventually its more descriptive name Harlech, or above the boulders. *Llech,* meaning huge stone, as in *cromlech.* In the vicinity of the castle there are places called the *Llech, Tan-y-Llech* and *Pen Llech,* hence *Ar-Lech* is undoubtedly the proper derivation."

"By order of the King (Edward IV.) William Herbert, Earl of Pembroke, led a powerful army to Harlech, and demanded the surrender of the place; but Sir Richard Herbert, the Earl's brother, received from the stout defender this answer—'I held a tower in France till all the old women in Wales heard of it, and now all the old women in France shall hear how I defend this castle.' Famine, however, at length succeeded, and the intrepid Welshman (*Dafydd ap Jevan*) made an honorable capitulation.—*Dr. Nicholas' Antiquities of Wales.*

WALLACHIA.
NATIONAL AIR.

By Boyard Nicolas Filipesco.

WALLACHIA.

YAP ISLAND.

AIR.

ZAMBOANGA ISLAND.

TYPICAL AIR.

ZANZIBAR.

THE SULTAN'S OR NATIONAL AIR.

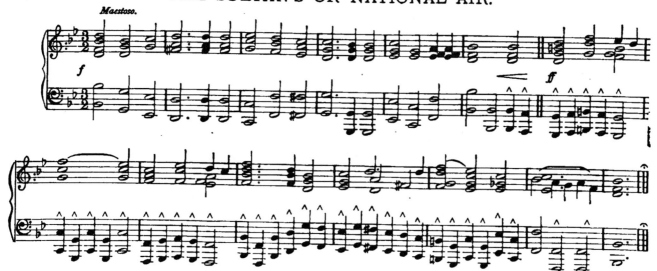

CPSIA information can be obtained at www.ICGtesting.com
Printed in the USA
LVOW092019230912

299701LV00007BB/1/P